Collins

Student Support Materials for **AQA**

A-level
Sociology

Crime and Deviance with Theory and Methods

Authors: Steve Chapman and Judith Copeland

HarperCollins
PUBLISHERS
Since 1817

Published by Collins
An imprint of HarperCollins*Publishers*
The News Building
1 London Bridge Street
London
SE1 9GF

Browse the complete Collins catalogue at
www.collins.co.uk

Commissioned by Catherine Martin

Developed by Jo Kemp

Project managed by Sadique Basha at Jouve India Private
Limited

Copyedited by Lucy Hyde

Proofread by Nikky Twyman

Original design by Newgen Imaging

Typeset and Indexed by Jouve India Private Limited

Cover design by Ink Tank

Cover image by sysasya photography/Shutterstock

Production by Lauren Crisp

Printed and bound by Martins the Printers

Acknowledgements

Every effort has been made to contact the holders of
copyright material, but if any have been inadvertently
overlooked the publishers will be pleased to make the
necessary arrangements at the first opportunity.

p11, table 2, source: Health and Safety Executive, 1995;
p30, study, source: Home Office Crime Statistics; p31,
study, source: Offending, Crime and Justice Survey 2003,
Home Office; p52, study, source: Rob White, 'Green
Criminology and the Pursuit of Social and Ecological
Justice', eds. P. Bierne & N. South, *Issues in Green
Criminology* (2007), Devon: Willan Publishing; p44, study,
source: Keith Soothill and Sylvia Walby, *Sex Crime in the
News* (2001), Routledge; p44, source: Jason Ditton and
James Duffy, 'Bias in the Newspaper Reporting of Crime
News', *British Journal of Criminology* (1983), 23 (2),
159–165, Oxford University Press; p60, study, source: HM
Prison Service.

Thanks to Peter Langley for his work as series editor on
the first edition.

Contents

Chapter 1: Theories of crime and deviance 4–35

Functionalist explanations of crime and deviance; Subcultural explanations of crime and deviance; Marxist explanations of crime and deviance; Neo-Marxist explanations of crime and deviance – the 'New Criminology'; Interactionist explanations of crime and deviance; Right Realist explanations of crime and deviance; Left Realist explanations of crime and deviance; Explanations of gender differences in crime rates – feminism; Explanations of gender differences in crime rates – masculinity; Explanations of ethnic differences in crime rates; Explanations of class differences in crime rates

Chapter 2: The social distribution of crime and deviance 36–43

Recent trends and patterns in crime – the official crime statistics; Problems of reliability and validity of crime statistics

Chapter 3: Globalization and crime in contemporary society 44–55

The mass media and crime; Globalization and crime; Green crime; Human rights and state crime

Chapter 4: Crime control, prevention and punishment 56–63

Control and prevention of crime; The victims of crime

Chapter 5: Theory and methods 64–101

Functionalism and consensus theory; Marxism and conflict theory; Feminism; Social action theory; Modernity and postmodernity; Positivist research methods; Sampling; Interpretivist research methods; Sociology and science; Sociology and values; Sociology and social policy

Chapter 6: Exam practice 102–118

Glossary 119–125

Index 126–128

Functionalists argue that crime and deviance can only be explained by looking at the way societies are organized socially – their **social structures** – and that crime is caused by society rather than by the circumstances of the individual. Functionalism is therefore a **structuralist theory** of crime.

Émile Durkheim

Émile Durkheim believed that the crime rates of pre-industrial societies were very low because their social structures were characterized by 'mechanical solidarity'. This means that both family and religion were powerful agencies of socialization and **social control**. These agencies were extremely influential in bringing about a powerful **consensus** about right and wrong behaviour, and an acceptance that those who committed crime and deviance deserved severe punishments such as the death penalty. Moreover members of pre-industrial societies saw individuality as potentially deviant, because they had been socialized into putting their community before self-interest. In contrast, Durkheim argued that crime rates are higher in modern societies because the social structures of these societies are characterized by 'organic solidarity'. In these highly urbanized and impersonal societies, the authority of religion and family have grown weak as belief systems, such as science and other political and philosophical ideologies, have appeared, and challenged religious authority and promoted **individualism**. Consequently, in modern urban societies, **value consensus**, community duties and obligations and social controls or punishments have grown weaker as people have grown more egoistic or individualistic. For example, in many Western societies, the death penalty has been abolished and liberal attitudes about previously forbidden behaviour such as homosexuality are common. Durkheim argued that people in such societies are more likely to experience **anomie** – a sense of moral confusion that weakens their commitment to shared values and rules and which no longer deters or discourages criminal or deviant behaviour.

Durkheim observed that crime and deviance are present in all societies. He argued that the basis of social order in society was a set of shared values (value consensus) or collective conscience. The collective conscience provides boundaries, which distinguish between actions that are acceptable and those that are not. The problem for modern societies is that these boundaries are no longer clear, and also that they change over time. Durkheim believed that crime, or at least a certain limited amount of crime, **functions** for the benefit of society because its existence both maintains and clarifies the boundaries between legal and illegal behaviour as well as promoting boundary adaptation and change. This can be illustrated in three ways:

- **Reaffirming the boundaries** – Every time a person breaks a law and is taken to court, the resulting court case and media publicity reaffirms existing values and boundaries. This is particularly clear in societies where public punishments take place – for example, where a murderer is taken out to be executed in public or an adulterer is stoned to death. The pursuit, trial and public punishment of criminals therefore reassures people that society is functioning effectively, while reminding them of the acceptable social boundaries of behaviour.

- **Changing values** – On occasion some individuals or groups deliberately set out to defy laws which they believe are wrong. Acts of crime and deviance can provoke positive social change by highlighting aspects of the social structure, collective conscience or the law that are inadequate or outdated. People who commit crime for this reason are often ahead of their time and can be termed functional rebels because they help to change the collective conscience and laws based on it for the better, anticipating and helping to produce social changes which help society function more effectively. Examples of functional rebels might include groups such as the Suffragettes, and individuals such as Rosa Parks, Martin Luther King and Nelson Mandela. Gay rights campaigners such as Peter Tatchell have deliberately broken laws regarding public displays of homosexuality so that the collective conscience has grown more tolerant of same-sex relationships, and laws have adapted by decriminalizing homosexuality. In October 2016 the UK Ministry of Justice announced that all gay and bisexual men convicted of obsolete homosexual offences are to pardoned, whether alive or dead.

- **Social cohesion** – Durkheim points out that horrific crimes such as child murders or terrorism create shared outrage which reinforces community solidarity. This was particularly noticeable, for example, in the UK following the July 2005 London Underground bombings and in France following the terrorist attacks in Paris in November 2015 and Nice in July 2016.

Evaluation of Durkheim

- He never explains why certain social groups – the poor, young people, males – commit crime. His explanation for rising crime is rather vague – anomie caused by rising levels of egoism. It is not clear how these concepts are practically converted into particular criminal actions.
- He neglects the fact that some crimes – for example, rape, child abuse and terrorism – are always **dysfunctional** for their victims.
- Marxists argue that he exaggerates the degree of consensus in societies and underestimates the level of conflict and inequality in modern societies, which they argue is the most likely cause of crime.
- Tim Newburn criticizes Durkheim because he neglects the role of the powerful in shaping the consensus about what is criminal and what is normal practice. For example, many of the 'sharp' practices of bankers that many people clearly see as immoral are not actually illegal because the wealthy can put pressure on lawmakers to ensure that their norms are not outlawed.
- Nevertheless, Durkheim's theory has been extremely influential and inspired other theories of crime and delinquency; particularly those of Merton and Cohen.

Essential notes

Illustrate how boundaries adapt and change by researching how gay rights campaigners broke outdated laws with, for example, mass 'kiss-ins'. Another example worth investigation is the Fathers4Justice campaign.

☞ This topic continues on the next two pages

Robert Merton

Robert Merton argued that the cause of crime lies in the relationship between the culture and the social structure of society. In capitalist societies, cultural institutions such as the mass media socialize individuals into believing that material success is a realistic goal for all.

However, Merton noted that the institutional means required to achieve the goal of material success (the educational system in the form of qualifications, and the economic system in the form of well-paid jobs), are not fairly distributed in capitalist societies. For Merton, crime and deviance were evidence of a poor fit (or a **strain**) between the socially accepted cultural goals of society, and the socially approved means – education and jobs – of obtaining those desired goals. In other words, some social groups, particularly the children of the poor, did not enjoy the same access to education and jobs as the children of the wealthy. The USA was not the level playing field that American culture claimed it was. Merton believed that the resulting strain between culture and the institutional means of achieving material success led to people experiencing a state of anomie, which he defined as a form of frustration and disenchantment. Merton argued that individuals could respond to anomie by adopting one of five different forms of behaviour or adaptations, as outlined in Table 1.

Essential notes

Merton's theory can be applied to most Western capitalist economies, including the UK. Think about how the cultural goals of the UK are organized around the interrelated values of monetary success, celebrity, consumerism and materialism.

Essential notes

Think about how a sociologist might research the validity of Merton's ideas. What sample of people could be used to research whether people are suffering from anomie and adopting these responses? What method might a positivist sociologist prefer, compared with an **interpretivist sociologist**?

Essential notes

Use examples whenever possible to illustrate Merton's 5 responses. For example, research modern day terror groups such as IS to work out whether they fit Merton's description of rebels.

Response	Method of individual's response
Conformity	Most of the population cope by doing their best and making the most of what society offers them. They remain committed to both goals and means despite little likelihood of success.
Innovation	Commitment to cultural goals may remain strong, but a small section of the working class reject the conventional means of acquiring material success and turn to criminal means to achieve wealth. For example, organized crime, particularly that related to the buying and selling on of Class A drugs such as heroin, is estimated to be worth millions of pounds for those involved.
Ritualism	Some people lose sight of material goals, but derive satisfaction from fairly meaningless jobs, for example, the bureaucrat who goes through the motions of doing their job but has given up on the possibility of promotion and the prospect of ever being wealthy or powerful.
Retreatism	A small number of people reject both the goals and means by dropping out of 'normal' society entirely. Instead, they may become dependent on welfare benefits, alcohol or drugs.
Rebellion	People may rebel and seek to replace mainstream goals and institutional means with more radical alternatives, and may use violent methods to achieve this.

Table 1
Responses to anomie

Merton concludes that criminals are not that different from law-abiding citizens. They have been socialized into the the same cultural goals as everyone else but realise that crime is their only means of achieving material success.

Evaluation of Merton

- Merton does not explain why some individuals commit crime, whilst others conform, retreat or rebel.
- Merton's theory explains crime that results in economic gain, but he does not explain many forms of violent and sexual crimes.
- He also fails to explain crimes committed by young people in gangs, which do not seem to be motivated by material goals.
- Valier (2001) points out that it is rare that people strive for only one cultural goal. He argues that people tend to set themselves a variety of goals. For example, people might prioritize doing good or constructing a healthy work/leisure balance or making sure that they attain a happy family life over material success and power.
- White-collar and **corporate crime** arise from access to opportunities rather than the blocking of them. Thus, he probably underestimates the amount of crime committed by the upper and middle classes.
- As a functionalist, Merton assumes that the law treats everybody equally. However, Marxists such as Box point out that the law is not neutral because it is constructed by the capitalist class in order to protect their interests.

However, Merton's theory has proved to be very influential. Some sociologists claim it still has contemporary relevance. Sumner claims that Merton has uncovered the main cause of crime in modern societies – the alienation caused by disillusionment with the impossible goals set by **capitalism**. Reiner (2015) claims that Merton's theory partly explains the 2011 London riots as well as the MP expenses scandal of 2009.

Essential notes

The American Dream is a cultural idea popular in the USA. It suggests that the USA practises equality of opportunity and, consequently, if a person is talented and willing to work hard, success should be forthcoming regardless of social background. Abraham Lincoln and Barack Obama, who both came from fairly modest social backgrounds, are cited as examples.

Examiners' notes

Successful evaluation is balanced evaluation – it should contain reference to the strengths as well as the weaknesses of particular studies or theories.

Essential notes

Be aware of the other theories that Merton influenced, especially Cohen's subcultural theory, Cloward and Ohlin's theory of illegitimate opportunity structure and Cashmore's theory as to why black youths might commit crime (see pp 14–15, 33–34).

Subcultural theory focuses on explaining why young working-class people commit crime. Known as **juvenile delinquency**, it is often malicious in nature and not linked to material or financial goals. Subcultural theory also tries to explain why juvenile delinquency has a collective or subcultural character – it is committed as part of a larger group or gang.

Albert Cohen

Albert Cohen was particularly interested in the fact that Merton had not really addressed juvenile delinquency. He observed that the type of crimes committed by children and teenagers tends to be of a non-utilitarian nature. This means that crimes such as gang violence, joy-riding, hooliganism, vandalism and anti-social behaviour have no obvious economic benefit to the offender. Cohen, like Merton, argues that delinquency is caused by a strain between cultural goals and the institutional means of achieving them. He suggests that young people aspire to the goals of status and respect. Middle-class youngsters usually attain status from their parents, teachers and peers as they achieve educational success. However, Cohen suggests that working-class boys are denied status at school, as their parents have failed to equip them with the skills they need to succeed. Thus, these boys are placed in the bottom sets and consequently are unable to acquire the status enjoyed by students in the higher sets. Such boys may leave school with few or no qualifications and then work in low-paid jobs or become unemployed. In this sense, they are denied status by wider society.

Cohen argues that these experiences result in low self-esteem. These boys feel alienated and angry at the low status that schools and society allocate them. They experience a form of anomie, which Cohen called '**status frustration**'. They respond by developing gangs or **subcultures** of like-minded boys who reverse the norms and values of the dominant culture and award one another status on the basis of anti-school and delinquent behaviour.

Evaluation of Cohen

- Paul Willis concludes that Cohen is wrong to assume that working-class youth share the same goals as middle class youth. The boys in Willis' study defined educational failure as 'success' because qualifications were not necessary for the types of factory jobs they wanted.
- Most working-class boys actually conform at school despite educational failure. They rarely commit to anti-school subcultures.
- Cohen ignores female delinquency, focusing entirely on working-class boys.
- He neglects the role of agencies of social control in the social construction of delinquency.

Walter Miller

Walter Miller suggests that working-class juvenile delinquency is not the result of strain or status frustration. Rather, he argues that working-class juvenile delinquents are merely acting out and exaggerating the mainstream values of working-class subculture. Miller suggests that working-class youth subculture has developed a series of '**focal concerns**', which give meaning to their lives outside work. These include a heightened sense of masculinity (which sees violence as an acceptable problem-solving device), a desire for excitement and being anti-authority. Living out these focal concerns compensates for the boredom of school or factory jobs. However, it may also cause confrontation with teachers and the police. Thus, Miller blames working-class delinquency on what he sees as the potentially deviant nature of working-class culture.

Richard Cloward and Lloyd Ohlin

However, Merton's ideas about strain had a very significant impact on the theory of Richard Cloward and Lloyd Ohlin, who argue that Merton failed to acknowledge that there existed a parallel opportunity structure to the legal one, called the **illegitimate opportunity structure**. They suggest that the type of crime committed by young people depends on the type of illegitimate opportunity structure that is available to them in their locality. They identify three types of illegitimate opportunity structures, which produce three different types of subcultural delinquent behaviour:

1. In some areas, there are established patterns of illegitimate opportunity in which people experience criminal 'careers'. These organized types of criminal subcultures mirror legitimate businesses, in that employees have specific roles and can be promoted upwards to managerial or executive status. Sudhir Venkatesh observed such a subculture in Chicago in his study *Gang Leader for a Day*.
2. Some inner-city areas may be dominated by conflict subcultures, which engage in highly masculinized territorial or respect-driven violence. It was estimated by the police in 2012 that there were 250 active gangs in London involving 4800 people.
3. If young people fail to gain access to either the criminal or conflict subcultures, they may form retreatist subcultures, in which the major activities are recreational drug use. There is some evidence that subcultures of heroin addicts may be responsible for the majority of crimes such as street robbery, burglary and shoplifting carried out in inner cities in order to raise the cash needed to finance their addiction.

Criticisms of subcultural theory

David Matza, an interactionist sociologist, suggests that subcultural theories have the following problems:

- Only a minority of young people actually get into trouble with the police or join territorial street gangs.
- Young people may drift in and out of delinquency but they eventually grow out of it when they reach adulthood.
- When talking about their delinquency, young people rarely reference status frustration or the strain involved attempting to achieve material success or even belief in a set of deviant subcultural values.
- **Labelling theory** is critical of subcultural theorists such as Cohen, Cloward and Ohlin, and Miller because they all neglect the role of the police. Police may target and label or **stereotype** young working-class people as potentially criminal and frequently stop, search and arrest them, whereas they may ignore similar behaviour demonstrated by middle-class youth because it does not fit the police's interpretation of what constitutes criminal or delinquent behaviour. Working-class criminality may therefore be socially constructed by police practices and interpretations rather than be the result of a strain between culture and structure.
- Matza argues that most people subscribe to subterranean values - they crave excitement and thrills and wish to take risks. Most social groups can legitimately express these values (e.g. through sport) but because powerless groups are under surveillance, when they attempt to turn these subterranean values into practice, they are more likely to be labelled delinquent or criminal.

Essential notes

You should think about the strengths and limitations of this type of research.

Essential notes

Although Miller's theory is subcultural, it bears little resemblance to Cohen's theory, which partly blames society for gang activity. Miller strongly implies that working-class culture is problematic and inferior compared to middle-class culture. His theory is not dissimilar to the '**underclass**' theory of Charles Murray.

Examiners' notes

Venkatesh's study is a good example of **participant observation**. Study it in some detail so that you can clearly recognize the strengths and limitations of this research method in the study of gangs. Compare it with UK research into gangs that has used participant observation, especially James Patrick's *A Glasgow Street Gang Observed*, which used a covert form of participant observation. When evaluating a study you can also evaluate the research method used alongside the significance of the study and the target focus of the question.

Marxists argue that the very nature and organization of capitalism is **criminogenic** – the values that underpin capitalism encourage criminal behaviour in all social classes. Marxists therefore believe that crime is inevitable within capitalist societies. This can be illustrated in two main ways.

1. David Gordon argues that capitalism is characterized by class inequalities in the distribution of, for example, wealth and income. Consequently, poverty, unemployment, low-quality housing or homelessness, debt and foodbanks. are 'normal' facts of life for those at the bottom end of capitalist society. Gordon suggests that crime committed by the poor, the homeless and the unemployed is actually a realistic and rational response to the inequalities and humiliations they experience on a daily basis. In societies with inadequate welfare provision, such as the USA, Gordon argues that crime may be necessary for survival. Gordon argues that, considering the nature of capitalism, sociologists should not ask 'Why do the working class commit crime?' but instead 'Why don't they commit more crime?'

2. William Chambliss argued that capitalism is based upon competition, selfishness and greed, and this shapes people's attitudes to life. Similarly, Gordon argues that the **ideology** of capitalism encourages criminal behaviour in all social classes; for example, he argues that capitalism encourages a 'dog eat dog' system of ruthless competition. Moreover, capitalist values such as individualism, materialism and consumerism have become more important than community, cooperation and altruism (the desire to help others), and the media's emphasis on celebrity, monetary value and material success has encouraged a common culture of greed and naked self-interest. In this criminogenic environment it is not surprising there is crime. The need to win at all costs or go out of business, as well as the need to make a profit and the desire for self-enrichment, encourage even the already rich and powerful to commit white-collar and corporate crimes such as tax evasion. The capitalist emphasis on wealth may also encourage a 'culture of envy' among poorer sections of society, who may respond to growing inequality with resentful casual violence.

The law as ideology and social control

Marxists, like Louis Althusser, argue that the law is an **ideological state apparatus**, which functions in the interests of the capitalist class to maintain and legitimate class inequality in the following ways:

- It is concerned mainly with protecting the major priorities of capitalism – wealth, private property and profit. Laureen Snider notes that the capitalist state is reluctant to pass laws that regulate the activities of businesses or threaten their profitability.
- Stephen Box notes that the powerful kill, injure, maim and steal from ordinary members of society but these killings, injuries and thefts are often not covered by the law. For example, a worker's death due to employer infringements of health and safety laws is a civil, rather

than criminal, offence. Employers and businesses that break such laws are rarely subjected to criminal prosecution or sent to prison, if found guilty.

- Sayer (2015) believes that the rich largely shape the law so that they do not end up in prison. For example, they make sure that governments do not close down loopholes which allow the rich and big companies to avoid tax. This includes allowing tax havens – small islands or states where money can be hidden or where tax rates are low.

- Law enforcement is selective and tends to favour the rich and powerful. For example, social security fraud, largely committed by the poor, inevitably attracts prosecution and often prison, yet tax fraudsters, who are usually wealthy and powerful individuals rather than ordinary taxpayers, rarely get taken to court if the tax authorities uncover evidence of such fraud. HM Customs and Excise are more likely to enter into a private arrangement with the individual in which he or she agrees to pay back the missing tax plus an additional surcharge or unofficial 'fine', although in 2015 the Government announced new criminal offences in an attempt to clamp down on corporate tax evaders.

- Jeffrey Reiman (2001) argues that the more likely a crime is to be committed by higher-class people, the less likely it is to be treated as a criminal offence. In particular, white-collar and corporate crimes are under-policed and under-punished.

White-collar and corporate crime

Marxists are particularly interested in crimes committed by the wealthy and powerful, such as white-collar and corporate crime. **White-collar crime** is defined as crime which involves the abuse of the trust and power associated with particular occupational roles, for example, an accountant or solicitor may use their privileged position to siphon funds out of a client's account without their permission or know. Croall identifies fraud, accounting offences, tax evasion and insider dealing as examples of white-collar crimes. She notes that people who own the means of production or who manage them have greater opportunities than most to make large sums of money from white-collar crime.

Croall notes that companies also commit crimes, known as corporate crimes. Examples are:

Type of crime	Example
Crimes against consumers	Manufacturing and selling dangerous goods or foods; not ensuring the safety of passengers
Crimes against employees	In the UK, between 1965 and 1995, 25,000 people were killed in the workplace; about 70% of these deaths were due to employer violation of health and safety laws
Environmental offences	Pollution of air and water, destruction of rainforests, illegal dumping of toxic waste
Financial fraud	False accounting; share price fixing, bribery and corruption

Essential notes

Marxists argue that capitalism is criminogenic – this means that it is a natural outcome of capitalist practices and values.

Essential notes

It is worth researching and studying a couple of examples of corporate crime in some depth. There is a wealth of information available on the internet about (a) the role of Union Carbide in the Bhopal disaster of 1984; (b) the thalidomide baby scandal of the late 1950s; (c) the Nestlé baby milk controversy reported in 1974; (d) the role of the National Coal Board in the Aberfan, Wales disaster of 1966 in which 144 people (including 116 children) died; (e) the banking crisis of 2008, which was caused by the legally dubious activities of several big banks in both the USA; and (f) the payment by BAE Systems of huge bribes to Saudi princes in return for arms orders in 2009.

Table 2
Examples of corporate crimes

☞ This topic continues on the next two pages

Essential notes

Think about how you would explain why people who are already rich and powerful might be motivated to commit crimes. The ideas of Gordon, functionalists and Left Realists might help.

Examiners' notes

White-collar and corporate crime is a difficult subject to research because of its nature and the fact that its perpetrators have the power to deny sociologists access to, for example, their offices, companies and staff. Primary research could be focused on the victims of specific types of white-collar or corporate crimes, but many sociologists working in this field are dependent on secondary sources. What **secondary data** might a sociologist use to investigate white-collar or corporate crime, and what are their strengths and limitations?

Croall argues that despite the fact that the costs of corporate and white-collar crimes far outstrip the overall combined annual value of burglary, theft and robbery, these types of crimes are not regarded as a serious problem by the general public for the following reasons:

- People do not fear white-collar or corporate crime in the same way as they do robbery or violence because these crimes are less visible than street crimes and hidden from the public gaze.
- Many of these crimes are complex, because they involve the abuse of technical, financial or scientific knowledge that the general public are unlikely to understand.
- It is difficult to identify which specific individuals are responsible for corporate crime because responsibility in big companies for specific actions is often unclear which makes it difficult to allocate blame.
- People may not realize that they have been victims of a corporate crime.
- Croall notes that there is often a very fine line between what are morally acceptable and unacceptable business practices. For example, nobody likes paying tax, so the general public might not view tax evasion as a serious problem.
- Many of the regulatory bodies, which monitor these types of crimes, advise and warn offenders rather than punish them. Corporate offenders are rarely taken to court.

Evaluation of traditional Marxism

- Unlike functionalism, it does not assume law is the product of consensus or that it benefits everyone. In contrast, it recognizes that the criminal justice system can be manipulated by powerful wealthy interests.
- Marxism was the first theory to question the functionalist idea that the law was an objective measure of 'harm' or 'wrong', and therefore 'just'. Marxist criminologists were the first sociologists to take a critical look at the law and the criminal justice system.
- Functionalists such as Merton see crime appearing when capitalism 'goes wrong'. In contrast, Marxists argue crime is endemic in capitalist societies because capitalist culture promotes criminogenic values and practices.
- Richard Wilkinson has provided **empirical** data that demonstrates a clear link between inequality and crime. In societies such as the USA and UK, which demonstrate very wide inequalities between rich and poor, crime rates are high. However, crime rates are relatively low in capitalist societies that demonstrate low levels of inequality, such as Sweden and Japan.
- Marxist criminology has forced sociologists to explore the wider social, economic and political factors which shape society, especially the idea that the law itself reflects differences in power between groups and that the law may represent powerful interests.

- It was generally assumed by sociologists such as Merton that crime was mainly committed by members of the working class or poorer sections of society. In contrast, Marxists highlight the importance of examining harmful activities committed by the powerful, and attempt to explain why these activities are not defined as illegal and are largely invisible to the public eye.
- Marxist criminology has been criticized by feminists for failing to explain why crime is mainly a male activity.
- Subcultural theory, labelling theory and **Left Realists** observe that Marxists fail to explain why crime is mainly committed by the young.
- Marxism fails to explain why, despite living in a criminogenic society, most people never break the law.
- Surprisingly, Marxism has little or nothing to say about the victims of crime, who are mainly drawn from the poorer parts of society.
- The Marxist view of the law can be criticized as one-dimensional, because it is nearly always seen as reflecting the interests of the dominant class. Consequently, Marxists may fail to appreciate the influence of public opinion on the construction of law – for example, Clare's law, which enables females to check the police record of their partners, was the result of a public campaign launched in the wake of the murder of Clare Wood, who was murdered by her ex-boyfriend in 2009 – or they fail to appreciate that there are laws which do not always support the interests of the capitalist class, such as equal opportunity or minimum wage laws.
- Marxists neglect the fact that the criminal justice system sometimes does act against the interests of capitalism – by prosecuting members of the capitalist class for criminal offences.

Essential notes

Research the idea that the powerful are sometimes prosecuted for breaking the law so you have examples to illustrate this important point. You could research the prosecution of MPs and peers in 2012 who were accused of fiddling their expenses or the prosecutions of the MPs Jeffrey Archer and Jonathan Aitken.

Neo-Marxists are sociologists who have been influenced by many of the ideas of traditional Marxism, which they combine with ideas from other approaches, such as labelling theory.

The 'New Criminology' of Ian Taylor, Paul Walton and Jock Young is the most well-known example of **neo-Marxism**. This generally agrees with the traditional Marxist analysis that:

- Capitalist society is based on exploitation and class conflict and characterized by extreme inequalities of wealth and power.
- The state makes and enforces laws in the interests of the capitalist class and criminalizes members of the working class.

However, Neo-Marxists are critical of traditional Marxism, which they argue is too deterministic. For example:

Traditional Marxists	See the working class as the passive victims of capitalism, who are driven to criminality by factors beyond their control
Neo-Marxists	See the working-class as active agents who have free will and who voluntarily choose to commit crime as a political response to their negative experience of capitalism

Examiners' notes

The Theory and Method exam question may ask you to compare structuralist approaches with social action theories. The New Criminology combines structuralist Marxism with aspects of **social action theory**, that is, the idea that people experience and interpret the world around them and make choices as to how they should react.

Table 3
Example of the difference between traditional Marxism and neo-Marxism

Essential notes

The neo-Marxist theory sees working-class criminals as politically motivated by their negative experience of capitalism. It presents criminals as 'Robin Hoods' – stealing from the rich and redistributing to the poor. Some sociologists, most notably Paul Gilroy, have suggested that young black criminals are politically motivated to commit crime by their discovery of the history of slavery and colonialism as well as by their everyday experience of racism and police harassment.

From a neo-Marxist perspective, crime is a deliberate and meaningful political response by the powerless to their position within the capitalist system. The poor and the powerless commit crime as a way of protesting against injustice, exploitation and alienation. Neo-Marxists claim that crimes against property, such as theft and burglary, are a reaction to wealth inequality. Vandalism is a symbolic attack on society's obsession with property. Criminals are therefore not the passive victims of capitalism – they are actively struggling to alter capitalism and to change society for the better.

Neo-Marxists argue that the ruling class is aware of the revolutionary potential of working-class crime and has taken steps to control it. State apparatuses such as the police deliberately target and 'occupy' working-class areas, while the state has introduced 'repressive' laws such as the Criminal Justice Acts, which aim to control potential 'problem' populations such as the young, ethnic minorities and striking workers. Stuart Hall argues that the mainstream media also serves the interests of the ruling class. He claims that that the tabloid media in the 1970s deliberately (in collaboration with the police) reported 'mugging' or street robbery as a racial crime in which black criminals were presented as robbing mainly white victims. Hall claimed that this had the **ideological function** of dividing the black and white working class and setting them against each other. The resulting racial tension not only divided the working class but also diverted their attention away from the serious mismanagement of capitalism in this period by the ruling class.

Taylor, Walton and Young attempted to produce what they called a 'fully social theory of deviance', which identified six key questions that they argued need to be answered in order to understand crime and society's response to it:

1.	How is the crime linked to inequality?
2.	What particular social or economic situation led to the criminal or deviant act?
3.	How does the offender interpret the crime – do they apply a particular meaning to their motive for criminality?
4.	How do those close to the criminal such as family and community react to the crime and the offender?
5.	What is the relationship between crime and power? For example, who decides that some types of deviance should be treated more harshly than others?
6.	How do offenders react to being labelled criminal or deviant?

Evaluation of the 'New Criminology'

- Left Realists (see pp 24–25) have criticized the New Criminology for over-romanticizing working-class criminals as 'Robin Hoods' who are fighting capitalism by stealing from the rich and giving to the poor.
- The reality of crime is that most victims of working-class and black crime are themselves working class and black, and often poor. It is suggested that Taylor et al. do not take the effects of this type of crime on working-class victims seriously.
- Although some crimes are obviously political – for example, assassinations of politicians, terrorism, animal rights protesters' breaking into laboratories to free animals being experimented upon, and so on – it is difficult to imagine a political motive underpinning crimes such as domestic violence, rape and child abuse.
- Some criminologists argue that most crime is opportunist and committed on the spur of the moment rather than an attempt to right some perceived injustice. The New Criminology is often accused of being naive in its portrayal of criminality because it fails to consider that some criminals are simply 'bad' people.
- Roger Hopkins Burke (2005) concludes that both Marxist and Neo-Marxist theories are too general to explain crime and too idealistic. For example, these critical theories argue that crime can be eventually eradicated only if capitalism is made more 'caring' and less criminogenic, if class inequalities disappear and if the power of the capitalist class to make laws and to criminalize actions they find threatening is reduced. However, it is unclear how these solutions could be practically implemented.

Examiners' notes

Think about the type of research that could be designed to test the validity of the New Criminology. What research methods could be adopted? What sort of sample should be used? Why might newspaper reports from the 1970s relating to street robberies be inadequate to support Hall's notion of **moral panics** being used to divide the working class?

Examiners' notes

Be aware of how the two types of Marxism – traditional and the New Criminology – are related, but make sure you gain marks for evaluation by clearly identifying their differences.

Examiners' notes

Theory and Method exam questions may require you to compare social action theories such as **interactionism** (short term for **symbolic interactionism**) with structural theories. You should know how interactionists or social action theory explain the organization of societies like the UK compared with structural theories such as functionalism and Marxism. Also, you should be able to use the interactionist theory (also known as labelling theory) of crime and/ or education to illustrate aspects of the social action theory of society. Be aware, too, that some theories combine elements of both structuralist and social action theories, such as the 'New Criminology'.

Essential notes

The concept of social construction is very important, as it suggests that those who are defined and labelled as criminals are the victims of those with power, who disapprove of their behaviour. This strongly implies that people who are labelled criminals or deviants are not responsible for their deviance – rather, that the label is the product of power inequalities.

Interactionist approaches to crime and deviance belong to the interpretivist or social action theory tradition, which is interested in how people interpret and therefore socially construct the world around them. They are also interested in looking at how criminality develops in the social interactions between a potential deviant and agents of social control, such as police officers.

The relativity of deviance

Interactionists believe that 'normality' and 'deviance' are relative concepts, because there is no universal or fixed agreement on how to define them. They point out that definitions of 'right' or 'wrong' behaviour differ according to social context. For example, nudity is fine in the privacy of the bathroom or bedroom but may be interpreted as a symptom of mental illness or criminality if persistently carried out in public.

Definitions of deviance change according to historical period; for example, homosexuality and suicide were defined as illegal activities until the 1960s. The definitions also change according to the cultural or subcultural context; for example, drinking alcohol is illegal in Saudi Arabia and disapproved of by Muslims in the UK.

The interpretation of deviance

Interactionists believe that deviance is therefore a matter of interpretation. For example, society generally disapproves of killing people, although certain types of 'killing', such as capital punishment or shootings by police officers, are interpreted very differently from other types of killing, such as murder or manslaughter. Killing enemy soldiers in wartime is actually regarded as an heroic action which may be rewarded with medals. In 2012, the government announced that those who kill burglars in defence of their families and property are unlikely to be prosecuted.

The social construction of deviance

Howard Becker argues that there is no such thing as a deviant act because no act is inherently criminal or deviant in itself, in all situations and at all times. Instead, it only becomes criminal or deviant only when others label it as such.

Becker therefore argues that the social construction of deviance requires two activities. One group, which lacks power, acts in a particular way. Another group, with more power, responds negatively to it and defines and labels it as criminal. Therefore, for Becker, a deviant is simply someone to whom a label has been successfully applied, and deviant behaviour is simply behaviour that people have labelled as such.

Becker notes that powerful groups create rules or laws in order to define what counts as crime and deviance, and label those who fail to conform to these social controls as criminals or outlaws (outsiders).

The agents of social control

Becker notes that the agents of social control are made up of groups who make up the criminal justice system such as the police, magistrates and judges social workers and probation workers. They work on behalf of politically powerful groups to label and thus define the behaviour of less powerful groups as being a problem. Consequently, the behaviour of the less powerful is subjected to greater surveillance and control by these social agencies.

The negotiation of justice

Interactionists argue that some groups have the power to avoid having negative labels applied to their behaviour. Cicourel concluded that justice is often not fixed but negotiable. For example, in his study of delinquency, he observed that when a middle-class youth was arrested, he was less likely to be charged with a criminal offence because his social background did not fit the police's stereotypical label of a 'typical' delinquent, but also because his parents were able to negotiate successfully on his behalf. They were more able than working-class parents to convince agents of social control that they would monitor him to make sure he stayed out of trouble. As a result he was 'counselled, warned and released', whilst working-class youths up for the same offences were charged with a criminal offence. Similarly, it may be the case that white-collar criminals may have the power to negotiate their way out of a criminal charge when dealing with agencies such as HM Customs and Excise.

Primary and secondary deviance

Edwin Lemert distinguishes between **primary deviance** and **secondary deviance**. Primary deviance refers to insignificant deviant acts that have not been publicly labelled. Such acts have little significance for a person's status or identity and, as a result, primary deviants do not see themselves as deviant.

Secondary deviance is the result of societal reaction – of labelling. Being caught and publicly labelled as a criminal can involve being **stigmatized**, shunned and excluded from normal society. The criminal label can become a **master status**, which means that society interprets all actions and motives in the context of the label. For example, if a person is labelled a 'sex offender', this label shapes people's reactions than any other status the person has.

Secondary deviance is likely to provoke further hostile reactions from society such as prejudice and discrimination. For example, people with criminal records may find it difficult to find a job or to rent or buy property. However, the practical consequences of treating a person as a deviant may produce a **self-fulfilling prophecy** because the labelled person may see him- or herself as deviant and act accordingly because they are isolated

Essential notes

Interactionists are very critical of the official criminal statistics (OCS), which they argue are also a social construction. They suggest that the OCS tell us more about the groups involved in their collection, especially victims, the police and the courts, than they tell us about crime and criminality (see pp 36–42).

Essential notes

Interactionist studies of crime have focused on how certain groups have come to be labelled as deviant by agents of social control such as the police and the mass media, and how such groups have reacted to the negative labels that have been applied to them. For example, Simon Holdaway's **covert participant observation** (conducted when he was a serving police officer) clearly shows that police officers negatively label and discriminate against particular groups, notably ethnic minorities, and that this stereotyping may be responsible for their disproportionate appearance in the OCS.

☞ This topic continues on the next two pages

Essential notes

The concept of power is central to the interactionist analysis. However, Marxists are critical of this theory, because interactionists are vague about the source of this power. Marxists argue that the power to label groups as criminal or deviant arises from the organization of capitalist society.

Examiners' notes

It is worth finding and studying key interactionist studies such as Howard Becker's *Becoming a Marihuana User* (1953) firsthand to understand more fully how social processes such as deviancy amplification occur.

from their 'normal' social contacts (family, friends and neighbours, work colleagues and so on) and because they are likely to seek comfort, sympathy, normality and status amongst those branded with similar labels – a subculture of deviants. This may help compensate for negative societal reaction but it also creates the potential for further deviance and even a **deviant career**, as the deviant subculture is likely to offer both the temptation and the opportunity to commit further deviance.

Deviancy amplification

'**Deviancy amplification**' is the term that labelling theorists use to describe the process in which the official attempt to control deviance or crime leads to an increase in the level of deviance. The term was coined by the British sociologist Les Wilkins in order to show how the response to deviance, by official agencies – such as the police and courts but also the tabloid media can actually generate an increase in crime and deviance.

According to Wilkins (1964), when people and certain acts are defined as deviant, the social group identified as 'deviant' are stigmatized and cut off from mainstream society. The social reaction to their behaviour – expressed by increased police use of **stop and search**, the flooding of the areas in which they live with more police officers and negative publicity about their behaviour in newspapers – makes the group more aware of their deviant identity and contributes to a self-fulfilling prophecy, in that members of the subculture become highly secretive in their activities. This provokes further official suspicion and even greater attempts to control the group and its activities. This, in turn, produces even higher levels of deviance in an escalating spiral or snowball process. In this sense, therefore, labelling theory argues that deviance can be caused by agencies of social control.

Evaluation of labelling theory

- Labelling theory has shown that defining deviance is a complex rather than a simple process.
- It has shown that definitions of deviance are relative and therefore not fixed, universal or unchangeable.
- Labelling theory was the first theory to draw sociological attention to the consequences of being labelled a deviant.
- Labelling theory shows that society's attempts to control deviance can sometimes backfire and create more deviance rather than less.

However:

- Labelling theory fails to explain the origin of deviance – it does not explain why people commit deviance in the first place, before they are labelled.
- Ronald Ackers argues that the deviant act is always more important than the societal reaction to it. He suggests that deviants know they are doing wrong and that their act is likely to result in a negative societal reaction.
- Labelling theory has been widely criticized for appearing to suggest that labelling inevitably leads to a deviant career.
- **Left Realists** argue that it is guilty of over-romanticizing deviant groups, neglecting their victims and blaming the agencies of social control for causing crime.

Examiners' notes

'Underclass' is a very loaded term and is therefore difficult to research (e.g. People are likely to admit to belonging to this group when filling in a questionnaire or when responding to an interview question). The theory is criticized for failing to provide convincing evidence for the existence of this subculture. Questionnaire surveys aimed at the poor suggest that with regard to jobs, they subscribe to the same types of beliefs as most other people, and that unemployment, poverty and debt have a negative effect on self-esteem and health.

Essential notes

Think about how Charlesworth's study of Rotherham might be used to criticise Murray's concept of the underclass.

Right Realists see crime, especially street crime, as a real and growing problem that undermines social cohesion and destroys social communities. They believe that people are naturally selfish, individualistic and greedy creatures. Right Realists, therefore, assume that people are 'naturally' inclined towards criminal behaviour if it can further their interests and/or if there is little chance of being caught.

Types of Right Realism

There are three main aspects to Right Realist theories of crime.

1. Underclass theory

Charles Murray suggests that, both in the USA and the UK, a distinct lower-class subculture exists, below the working class – an underclass – which subscribes to deviant and criminal values rather than mainstream values and transmits this deficient culture to their children via socialization.

David Marsland argues that the welfare state is responsible for the emergence of this underclass because **welfare dependency** has undermined people's sense of commitment and obligation to support one another. People belonging to the underclass are allegedly work-shy, choosing not to work and allegedly prefer to live off state benefits.

Murray sees the underclass as generally lacking in moral values, especially commitment to marriage and family life. A large percentage of underclass children are brought up by single mothers who he claims are inadequate and irresponsible parents. Absent fathers mean that boys lack paternal discipline and male role models, so young males may turn to other, often delinquent, role models on the street and gain status through crime rather than supporting their families by doing a steady job. These young males are also generally hostile towards the police and authority.

As a result, Right Realists see this alleged underclass as the main cause of crime in recent years in inner-city areas and on council estates.

Key study

Simon Charlesworth's study of poverty in Rotherham

Simon Charlesworth used **ethnographic research** to investigate the effects of poverty and unemployment on people living on a council estate in Rotherham, South Yorkshire. He took a flat on the estate and used both participant observation and conversational interviews to document the daily lives of the poor. He found the following:

- Miserable economic conditions had a profound negative effect on people's physical and mental health.
- Many of the unemployed suffered from depression.
- Many felt robbed of identity and value because they had no job.
- Although some people were motivated by their conditions to commit crime, most did not.
- There were few signs of the anti-social underclass Murray identified.

2. Rational choice theory

Clarke (1980) argues that the decision to commit crime is a choice based on a rational calculation of the likely consequences. If the rewards of crime outweigh its costs, or if the rewards of crime appear to be greater than those of non-criminal behaviour, then people will be more likely to offend.

Right Realists argue that, currently, the perceived costs of crime are low, so the crime rate has increased. Criminals foresee little risk of being caught and they view punishment if they are caught as weak and ineffective.

3. Control theories

Travis Hirschi argues that people are generally rational in terms of their actions and choices – they weigh up the 'costs' and 'benefits' of their behaviour, and on this basis they make choices about their actions.

Hirschi also argues that most people do not commit crimes, as they have four controls in their lives. So the cost of crime (being caught and punished) outweighs the economic and personal benefits. These controls are:

1. **Attachment** – being committed to family relationships, which may be threatened by involvement in criminality
2. **Commitment** – people may have invested years in education, building up a career or business or home, all of which may be lost if a person is involved in crime
3. **Involvement** – people may be actively involved in community life (e.g. as volunteers, magistrates, parent governors at local schools); respect and reputation would be lost if they engaged in crime
4. **Belief** – people may have been brought up to be strongly committed to beliefs in rules, discipline and respect for others and the law

Hirschi suggests that these controls prevent many people from turning to crime. As people get older, they begin to acquire these controls. Younger people usually have less to lose in terms of things like attachment. For them, respect and reputation might even be enhanced by criminality.

Evaluation of Right Realism

- John Rex and Sally Tomlinson reject the idea of the underclass as a deviant subculture that is voluntarily unemployed and devoted to criminal behaviour. They point out that poverty is often caused by factors beyond the control of the poor, for example, globalisation and government policies.
- There is no convincing empirical evidence that the underclass as a distinct subculture with distinctive values and behaviour exists.
- Right Realism overstates the rationality of criminals. For example, it is doubtful whether violent crime is underpinned by rationality.

Essential notes

Like Durkheim, Hirschi is more interested in *why* most people conform. Consequently, his theory is more about social control than about criminality. However, his theory implies that young people, ethnic minorities and members of the underclass are more likely to commit crime because they are more likely to lack these four controls.

Examiners' notes

Hirschi's ideas suffer from a lack of empirical evidence to support them. Think about how questionnaires or interviews might be designed and used to investigate the validity of these ideas.

Examiners' notes

Think about a comparative approach – what two groups might be selected to take part in this research? How might we **operationalize** Hirschi's concepts of attachment, commitment, involvement and belief?

☞ **This topic continues on the next two pages**

Right Realist schemes to prevent and control crime

- Murray favours less **social policy**. He suggests a reduction in state spending on welfare benefits in order to encourage members of the underclass to get jobs.
- Clarke, Hirschi and others have championed an anti-crime social policy known as '**situational crime prevention**' (SCP). This refers to measures aimed at reducing the opportunities for crime in any given situation. SCP social policies therefore focus on increasing the costs or risks so that the benefits of crime are significantly reduced. SCP includes:

  (a) **designing out crime or target hardening** – The New Right is very keen on the individual taking more responsibility for their welfare and homes. In their view, it is the responsibility of the householder, the car owner and businesses to take action against the criminal by designing crime out of their lives by investing in more security systems, such as locks for doors and windows, surveillance cameras and the installation of alarms and security lights. Individuals are encouraged by New Right sociologists to make themselves harder targets. All these things will increase the effort a burglar or thief needs to commit a crime and increase their risk of being caught and punished

  (b) **increased surveillance** – The UK has the highest number of CCTV cameras in the Western world – an estimated 4.2 million, which is one for every 14 people. New Right sociologists argue that such surveillance deters crime because it raises the potential cost of crime through increasing the chance of being caught.

Evaluation of situational crime prevention policies

- These strategies over-focus on opportunistic petty street crime and burglary, and ignore white-collar, corporate and state crimes, which are more costly and harmful.
- Violent crimes are often motivated drug addiction or gang membership and hyper-masculinity rather than rational thinking about the costs and benefits of crime.
- SCP ignores the root causes of crime, such as poverty and inequality.
- The use of surveillance may be a problem, because it may be used to infringe people's right to privacy.
- Evidence from Armstrong (1999) suggests that camera operators disproportionately focus on young males.
- Some criminologists argue that SCP strategies displace crime rather than reduce it. Criminals simply move to where the targets are softer. Burglars who are deterred by the security that characterizes middle-class homes will burgle the homes of people who cannot afford security.

Environmental crime control and prevention

The Right Realist James Wilson recommends a crime prevention social policy known as '**environmental crime prevention**' (ECP). Wilson argues that crime is caused by a decline in community controls and particularly neighbourhood disorder.

1. Wilson's theory of 'broken windows' argues that if signs of disorder, lack of concern for others and the decline of community or neighbourhood are allowed to develop, then crime rates rapidly increase. He suggests that symptoms of this disorder include the existence of anti-social behaviour, aggressive begging, drug dealing, drugs openly being used in public, drunkenness, graffiti, dog fouling, littering, vandalism and leaving broken windows unrepaired. Failure to deal with these problems immediately sends out a clear signal to criminals and deviants that no one cares, which encourages an increase in these problems.

2. All new public housing building by councils should not exceed three floors, and all residents should be encouraged to take collective responsibility for communal space in order to protect it from outsiders.

3. The police should adopt a **zero tolerance policing strategy** – instead of merely reacting to crime, they must aggressively tackle even the slightest signs of disorder; especially that concerning drugs and anti-social behaviour. Zero tolerance policing was famously adopted in New York in the 1990s to tackle crime and graffiti on the subway, fare dodging, drug dealing and begging, and led to a significant drop in crime (although critics question whether these crimes were the *result* of zero tolerance policing).

4. Other Right Realists argue for tougher punishments to deter crime. They argue that prison is effective in reducing crime because it firstly deters potential offenders away from crime. If an offender knows they are going to prison, the costs of crime clearly outweigh the benefits. An extreme example of this is California's 'three strikes and you are out' policy – in which criminals are imprisoned for life if convicted of a third offence, however serious or trivial this is. Secondly, prison incapacitates criminals, as it takes them off the streets for a sustained period. Thirdly, the New Right believe prison should truly be a punishment – it should be a form of retribution or pay-back and prisoners should feel they are being severely punished. The criminal justice system in the USA practices retributive justice. Some states have capital punishment and serving prisoners have to do 'hard labour', such as breaking rocks or working in the fields, as part of their prison programme.

Examiners' notes

Victim surveys are an important sociological method of collecting information about crime. You need to be aware of how the Islington Crime Survey was organized in terms of its methodology. Be aware of its strengths and weaknesses, especially compared with the British Crime Survey (BCS).

Essential notes

The concept of relative deprivation is important because it explains crime committed by a range of social groups (e.g. even white-collar crime can be explained using this concept). However, this concept is clearly related to Merton's ideas – note that both individualism and relative deprivation are linked to the functionalist idea that people's main cultural goal should be material success. The notion that individualism undermines community comes straight from Durkheim.

Essential notes

These ideas are not new – note how similar Lea and Young's concept of marginalisation is to Cohen's ideas about status frustration.

The Left Realists John Lea and Jock Young aim to explain street crime committed by young people in urban areas. Their **victim (or victimization) survey** of inner-city London (the Islington Crime Survey) suggested that working-class and black people, especially elderly women, have a realistic fear of street crime, because they reported that they are often the victims of such crime.

Lea and Young's explanation of why working-class and African-Caribbean young people commit crime revolves around three key concepts:

1. Relative deprivation

This refers to how deprived someone feels in relation to others, or compared with their own expectations. **Relative deprivation** can lead to crime when people feel resentment that, unfairly, others are better off than them. Lea and Young note that, although people today are more prosperous compared with the past, they are more aware of their relative deprivation because of media and advertising, which raise everyone's expectations about standards of living.

Left Realism argues that working-class youth feel relatively deprived compared to middle-class youth, while African-Caribbean youth compare themselves to white Britons with regard to life chances and opportunities such as living standards, access to consumer goods and income. These groups feel that they are relatively worse off through no fault of their own. For example, young black Britons may feel that racism is holding them back or blocking their opportunities to get ahead.

Feelings of relative deprivation are heightened when combined with individualism – the pursuit of self-interest – and are likely to lead to criminal responses because individualism undermines the family and community values of mutual support, cooperation and selflessness. The informal social controls usually exercised by the family and community are weakened. As a result, anti-social behaviour, violence and crime increase.

2. Marginalization

Left Realists argue that young people often feel **marginalized** (they feel they have little or no power to change their situation) and feel frustrated – negative treatment by the police and the authorities may result in further feelings of hostility and resentment towards mainstream society, which may spill over into confrontation with authority.

3. Subculture

Some young working-class and black people who experience these feelings of relative deprivation and marginalization may form deviant subcultures. These subcultures react to their perception that society does not value them by becoming involved in street crimes such as drug pushing, territorial gang violence, anti-social behaviour, joy-riding, rioting and mugging.

Left Realist solutions to crime

Left Realists argue that both the situational and environmental crime policies that Right Realists recommend are doomed to failure because they are treating the symptoms rather than the causes of crime. They argue that politicians need to remove the economic and social conditions that motivate groups such as the poor to commit crime in the first place. It is not enough to remove the opportunities for crime. Instead, we need to improve social conditions so that people are no longer motivated to look for criminal opportunities. Left Realists therefore recommend that government social policy should:

- reduce inequalities in wealth and income
- tackle educational underachievement, unemployment, low pay, discrimination and poverty
- improve housing and the environment of inner cities and council estates
- economically invest in poorer communities to create jobs
- attempt to regain the trust of local communities by reforming police – community relations by eradicating institutionally racist police practices such as racial profiling.

Evaluation of Left Realism

- Gordon Hughes argues that Left Realists have drawn our attention to the brutalizing and unromantic reality of inner-city street crime.
- They have also highlighted the effect of crime on victims.
- Left Realists have also shown clearly that most victims of crime are members of deprived groups – a fact which most theories of crime have neglected.

However:

- There is little empirical evidence to support the view that young working-class or black criminals interpret their realities in the way described by Lea and Young.
- Lea and Young do not explain why the majority of working-class and African-Caribbean youth do not turn to crime.
- The theory only focuses on subcultural criminal responses and does not explain crimes such as burglary, which is committed by individuals rather than gangs.
- It also focuses exclusively on street crime and largely ignores white-collar and corporate crime.
- It fails to account for opportunist crime committed by adults.

Essential notes

It is important to understand that subcultures do not have to be deviant. Some subcultures may be based around sport or religion, and channel feelings of frustration into positive areas.

Examiners' notes

Think about how these ideas might be researched. Lea and Young are suggesting that delinquents are motivated by the way they interpret the unequal socio-economic position they are in. Therefore, unstructured interviews, which are both flexible and focused on the research subject's interpretation of reality, might be the method that would generate the most valid or true-to-life data. The sample might be composed of teenage boys, convicted of delinquency, and might qualitatively explore their perceptions of materialism, deprivation and marginalization.

About 80% to 90% of offenders found guilty of or cautioned for committing crime are male. As a result, male crime is said to outnumber female crime by a ratio of 5 to 1. At least 33% of men are likely to be convicted for a criminal offence during their lifetime, compared with only 8% of women.

Men and women are convicted for different types of offences. For example, males dominate violent offences such as murder, and are 15 times more likely to be convicted for murder than women. Most female convictions are for property offences. Theft and handling stolen goods were most common female offences, accounting for 38% of all sentenced women in the year leading up to March 2013. In 2013, 26% of women in prison had no previous convictions, compared with only 12% of men.

Why women commit less crime than men

Some sociologists argue that the statistics are incorrect – women actually commit more crime than is officially acknowledged but are often treated more leniently by the police and the courts, so their crimes are less likely to be recorded, reported and prosecuted. Pollack argues that police culture (which is overwhelmingly male) is '**paternalistic**' and sexist. Females do not fit police stereotypes about 'suspicious' or 'criminal' behaviour, so females are less likely to be stopped, arrested or charged. Pollack and others have suggested that the police and courts treat female offenders more leniently. Pollack calls this 'softer' treatment the '**chivalry factor**'. Steffensmeier, too, argues that women are treated more leniently by the courts, because judges are reluctant to separate them from their children and regard them as less dangerous than men. Hood (1992) studied over 3000 court cases in which males and females were found guilty of similar crimes and found that women were a third less likely to be sent to prison.

Many feminist criminologists accept that women commit less crime than men. Six explanations try to explain the lower female crime rate:

1. Differential socialization
Both Carol Smart and Ann Oakley suggest that males are socialized into aggressive, self-seeking and individualistic behaviour that may make them more inclined to take risks and commit criminal acts. Diana Leonard believes that the major reason why women do not commit as much crime as men is that females are socialized into a culture of femininity that stresses communality cooperation, empathy and compassion for others. These values are more likely to deter criminal action.

2. Differential controls
Frances Heidensohn argues that females are generally more conformist because **patriarchal** society imposes greater control over their behaviour. This can be illustrated in a number of ways:

- Smart notes that girls are more strictly supervised by their parents, especially outside the home. Angela McRobbie and Jenny Garber concluded that teenage girls' lives revolve around a **bedroom culture**, so are more likely than boys to socialize with their friends at home rather than on the streets or in other public places.
- Sue Lees notes that girls fear acquiring a 'bad' reputation. She notes that boys in schools often use verbalized sexual labels such as 'slag' to control girls. Girls may steer clear of deviant behaviour in order to avoid these labels.

- Heidensohn notes that women are more likely to be controlled by their roles as wives and mothers, so have little time for illegal activity.
- Women are less likely to be in public places where crime and deviance normally occur, especially at night, because of the threat or fear of male violence or the fear of acquiring a bad reputation.

3. Crime as a rational choice

Pat Carlen argues that criminal women are often women who have failed to gain qualifications and find legitimate work. They often live in poverty and are dependent on benefits. Their attachment to family life may be weak because they have been abused by family members, run away from home and/or spent time in care. Many have lived rough on the streets. Carlen argues that many of these criminal women come to the rational conclusion that crime is the only route to a decent standard of living. Having a criminal record reinforces future criminal behaviour because it makes commitment to a conventional job and family life even less likely. However, critics of this theory suggest that Carlen fails to explain why many women in poverty choose *not* to commit crime.

4. The feminization of poverty

Some feminist sociologists suggest that poverty has become feminized in the last 20 years, as women have become increasingly more likely than men to experience low pay and benefits. Consequently, some types of crime dominated by females, notably shoplifting and social security fraud, may be a reaction to poverty. Sandra Walklate notes that shoplifting and prostitution are often motivated by economic necessity, for example, to provide children with food, toys and clothes.

5. Liberation theory

Freda Adler argues that as society becomes less patriarchal, so women's crime rates will rise. In other words, women's liberation from patriarchy may lead to a new type of female criminal because they will have greater opportunity and confidence to commit crime. For example, between 1981 and 1997, the number of under-18 girls convicted of violent offences in England and Wales doubled – from 65 per 100,000 to 135 per 100,000 (although male violence still far outstrips female violence).

Examiners' notes

Carlen conducted unstructured recorded interviews with 39 working women aged 15 to 46 who had been convicted of a range of crimes. At the times of the interviews, 20 were in custody. What problems of reliability might have occurred because of the method used? Why might the research design have produced high levels of validity in terms of the data generated by the interviews?

Examiners' notes

Self-report studies are a type of questionnaire used to investigate gender differences in committed crime. Campbell's self-report study found that the ratio of male crime to female crime is 1.5 to 1 rather than 7 to 1. However, the findings of such surveys are often undermined by over-reporting, under-reporting, ethical problems and the difficulty of finding a representative sample.

Essential notes

The empirical studies of territorial street gangs operating in UK cities in the 21st century by John Pitts and Keith Kintrea highlight the **hyper-masculine** aspect of gang culture focused on the search for respect and status, which they claim is responsible for much gun and knife crime in urban areas.

Examiners' notes

Student responses to essay questions on gender and crime tend to over-focus on the reasons why women do or do not commit crime. To maximize your marks, make sure you make reference to how male crime might be shaped by masculinity.

Until fairly recently, the idea that masculinity exerted a major influence on crime was generally neglected. Feminism was the first theory to draw criminological attention to the role of **gender-role socialization** in the social construction of crime. Oakley, for example, suggested that gender-role socialization in the UK, especially in working-class families, might result in boys and men subscribing to values that potentially overlap with criminality.

Oakley's ideas were developed by James Messerschmidt, who argued that boys in the UK are socialized into a **hegemonic** masculine value system that stresses differences from women, and particular masculine goals that need to be achieved in order to become a 'real man'. These goals include:

- the need to acquire respect from other men in order to maintain reputation
- having power, authority and control over others
- the **objectification of women** and the celebration of masculine virility through promiscuity
- toughness expressed through aggression, confrontation and force
- territorial loyalty and honour expressed through being part of a larger group or gang
- being emotionally hard and not expressing weakness by showing feelings
- being anti-authority, by claiming individuality and self-reliance
- taking risks and living life on the edge
- seeking pleasure, thrills and excitement to compensate for the boredom of work or unemployment.

However, Messerschmidt notes that the need to live out these masculine values is not confined to working-class youth and men. He notes that middle-class men may be motivated by this masculine value system to commit white-collar and corporate crime.

However Messerschmidt's analysis has been criticized because he fails to explain why not all men use crime to accomplish hegemonic masculine goals. The majority are law-abiding citizens.

Key study

Simon Winlow: The changing nature of masculinity

Winlow's study of masculinity in Sunderland suggests that most working-class men traditionally expressed their masculine values through the work they did, through their domestic roles as breadwinner and head of household and through their leisure time, which focused mainly on drinking in pubs. Opportunities to get involved in crime were fairly low, and violence, when it occurred, which was fairly rare, was shaped by masculine competition for respect and status or for the attention of women.

However, the mass unemployment of the 1980s experienced in industrial communities such as Sunderland meant that men could no longer express their masculinity through their work or by being the breadwinner. Economic change often meant that women became the breadwinners. Winlow notes that young men, in particular, experienced long-term unemployment after leaving school and became dependent on benefits. Winlow argues that these young men increasingly value violence, as it offers a release from boredom and access to status. In this world, the gang becomes all-important because it provides thrills, protection, mutual support, friendship, prestige, and income to buy fashionable clothes, alcohol and drugs.

Winlow suggests that the nature of criminal opportunity has also changed because of these economic changes. He argues that young men increasingly spend time building up their body capital by working out and 'pumping iron' at the gym because violence is now an **entrepreneurial concern** – a means of making money. Violent crime now offers a potential career path. For example, money can now be made:

- illegitimately, through protection rackets, dealing in drugs and/or stolen cars and loan sharking, which are crimes in which violence or the threat of it is a useful commodity
- legitimately, by being a bouncer on the door of a pub or club or a 'security consultant'.

Essential notes

Winlow used a combination of unstructured interviews and covert participant observation to study masculinity in Sunderland. He trained to be a bouncer and actually became a security doorman at a nightclub where he was able to observe masculinity firsthand. What do you think were the strengths and weaknesses of this approach?

Postmodern studies of masculinity and crime

Jackson Katz argues that young males commit crime for the pleasure or thrill that is derived from the risk of being caught or having power over others. Katz refers to these thrills as transgressions. Stephen Lyng suggests that much of crime is **edgework**, as it is located on the edge, between the thrill of getting away with it and the potential danger and uncertainty of being captured and punished. In this sense, crime is a form of gambling, providing pleasure and thrills. It allows young men who have little economic security to exercise a form of control over their lives. Katz also notes that violence, in terms of thrill and power exercised over others, is rational in the context of achieving the goals of hegemonic masculinity.

Essential notes

It is not just young males who are motivated by the excitement and danger associated with crime. Some criminologists, notably Croall, suggest female teenage crime might also be the product of this need for thrills.

African-Caribbean people and, to a lesser extent, Asian people are over-represented in the official crime statistics (OCS) and in the prison population.

The ethnic minority prison population has doubled in a decade – 25% of prisoners in 2015 came from ethnic minority backgrounds, up from 18% in 2009. Most of these prisoners are male. In 2015, 40% of 15- to 18-year-old boys held in youth custody in England and Wales were from ethnic minority backgrounds. Ethnic minority women are also over-represented in the criminal justice system. In 2009, 29% of the female prison population was made up of ethnic minority women. Muslims made up 14.6% of the prison population in 2015.

Sociological explanations of ethnic minority crime

Demographic explanations

Morris points out that most crime, according to the OCS, is committed by young people. He argues it is not surprising that there are a high number of black people in prison, because ethnic minority groups in the UK contain a disproportionate number of young people compared with the white population. However, this argument would be stronger if young Asians were also over-represented in prison (but they are not), as the majority of Asians in the UK are under 30 years old.

Interpretivist critiques of the criminal justice system

Interpretivist sociologists argue that criminal statistics do not tell us much about black or Asian criminality. Interpretivists suggest that the OCS are unreliable because they are socially constructed by the police and courts – they are not be a true record of ethnic minority crime. Rather interpretivists argue that the OCS may simply reflect levels of discrimination towards ethnic minorities by the police and other criminal justice agencies.

Coretta Phillips and Ben Bowling (2007) argue that, since the 1970s, the black community has been subjected to oppressive military-style policing, which has resulted in the over-policing of these communities, reflected in the excessive police use of stop and search. Statistics on police stop and search, released in 2015, reveal that police stop and search black Britons 4.2 times more than white Britons, and Asians twice as often as white Britons.

Various observational studies of police–suspect interaction suggest that the decisions of police officers to stop, search and arrest young African-Caribbean males are based on negative racial profiling or stereotyping. Simon Holdaway argues that police **canteen culture** is still characterized by racist language, jokes and banter and this racist culture often underpins the decision to stop black Britons. The MacPherson Report into the death of Stephen Lawrence, a black teenager, concluded that the London Metropolitan Police was guilty of **'institutional racism'** in its failure to tackle such discrimination. In 2008, the Metropolitan Black Police Association actually warned people from ethnic minorities not to join the police force because of what they perceived as a hostile and racist atmosphere at many London police stations.

Essential notes

It is important that you know how self-reports and victim surveys have been used to research the relationship between crime and ethnic minorities (see pp 62–63).

Key study

Waddington – police stop and search

P. A. J. Waddington et al. (2004) watched CCTV footage of police officers and interviewed officers about their stop-and-search activities.

They found that, although a disproportionate number of ethnic minority youth were stopped, this was a realistic reflection of the type of people who were on the streets at night in high crime areas.

In other words, police stop-and-search policies are not shaped by racial prejudice and discrimination, but by the composition of the local population.

Research indicates the possibility of some bias in the judicial process. C. Sharp and T. Budd observed in 2005 that young black Britons have lower offence levels compared to white youth, but are more likely to be arrested, taken to court and convicted. Furthermore, compared to white Britons, black and Asian offenders are more likely to be charged rather than cautioned, and remanded in custody rather than bailed. Hood's (1992) study of criminal courts in the West Midlands concluded that young African-Caribbean males were more likely than young white Britons to receive custodial sentences for the same types of offences.

Self-report studies such as the Offending, Crime and Justice Survey carried out in 2003 seem to support the view that the criminal justice system may be institutionally racist because they consistently show that white Britons have a higher rate of offending than black Britons. Moreover, those offences such as violence and drug-selling, which are stereotypically associated with black youth, are more likely to be committed by white youth.

Phillips and Bowling suggest that this negative treatment by the criminal justice system may lead some members of black communities to feel hostile towards the police. They note that young black Britons commit more street robbery than other ethnic groups and suggest that this is a product of the negative labelling that stems from constantly being stopped and searched by the police. Crime is an expression of the hostility they feel towards the police. In other words, police labelling produces a self-fulfilling prophecy, as young black Britons live up to the stereotype of potential criminals.

Examiners' notes

Think about the merits of using observation to study what goes on in courtrooms. How is such observation likely to be realistically organized? Think about the strengths and weaknesses of the observational method used by Hood, and Sharp and Budd.

Examiners' notes

If you are required to write a general essay on the merits of **interactionism** or labelling theory, you can use Phillips and Bowling's findings on the policing of ethnic minorities to illustrate the labelling process.

Key study

Cashmore – racism, blocked opportunities and anomie

Ernest Cashmore, using the ideas of Merton, argues that young African-Caribbeans in Britain are encouraged like everybody else to pursue material success, but their structural opportunities are blocked by racism, failing inner-city schools and unemployment. Young black Britons experience anomie – they are aware that their situation arises from being black in a mainly white society. They turn to street crime, which Merton described as 'innovation' (see p 6) – and justify their criminal activities on the grounds that they are rejecting white society because it has failed to offer them the opportunities that white Britons take for granted.

☞ This topic continues on the next two pages

Examiners' notes

You can use Cashmore's ideas to illustrate the functionalist theory society as well as the functionalist theory of crime and deviance.

Examiners' notes

You can use the work of Hall and Gilroy to illustrate either a 30-mark question on Marxist theory or one on Marxist explanations of crime and deviance.

Marxist and neo-Marxist explanations of crime committed by ethnic minorities

Marxists such as David Gordon point out that ethnic minorities often experience severe economic deprivation in terms of income and poverty as well as social deprivation in the form of living in deteriorating inner-city areas in poor-quality housing. In this sense, they are part and parcel of the working class, who may be motivated to commit crime because they are rationally reacting to conditions of inequality or because they have internalized the criminogenic values which are the natural outcome of living in a capitalist society underpinned by materialism and consumerism. Neo-Marxists such as Gilroy and Stuart argue that crime committed by young African-Caribbeans is political, as it is frequently motivated by their interpretation of their position in UK society. They argue that young black people voluntarily choose to commit crime as a form of symbolic protest against their historical exploitation and the everyday racism they experience on the streets from police officers.

However, the fact that the majority of young and adult African-Caribbeans are law-abiding citizens challenges the view that crime is part of an anti-colonial or anti-racist struggle. There is also no **empirical** evidence that black youths have the political motives that Gilroy identifies. Left Realists point out that most black crime is committed against other black people, rather than white people, which also undermines the neo-Marxist argument.

Stuart Hall on moral panic and the criminalization of young African-Caribbeans

The neo-Marxist Stuart Hall claims that the criminalization of black people began in the 1970s, when the police selectively released statistics suggesting that young black Britons were most likely to be responsible for street robbery or mugging, with white Britons likely to be the victims. This initiated a moral panic, which effectively labelled young African-Caribbean population as a **folk devil**, or criminal threat.

According to Hall, Britain in the early 1970s was undergoing a crisis of capitalism; unemployment was high, industrial disputes were common and riots, street protests and violent demonstrations threatened the cultural dominance, or **hegemony**, of the ruling capitalist class or **bourgeoisie**.

However, the moral panic focused on mugging came to play a crucial ideological function for the capitalist ruling class in two ways:

1. It divided the working class by encouraging racist attitudes – white working-class people were encouraged by the media, the police and politicians to view the black working class as a problem and threat. This distracted working-class members from the real cause of their problems – the mismanagement of capitalism by the ruling class.
2. It justified the introduction of more aggressive policing, particularly stop and search, and riot squads that could be used against other 'problem' groups such as strikers, protesters and demonstrators.

In Hall's view, the OCS, which show high levels of black criminality, are socially manufactured by a repressive racist state for ideological reasons.

Left Realism

Lea and Young attempted to explain street crime committed by both working-class white and black youth. They suggest that young black people feel relatively deprived when they compare themselves with young White people because they experience discrimination when applying for jobs and consequently are economically worse-off than their White peers. Furthermore they experience marginalization. They have little or no power to change their situation and feel frustrated and hostile because they are targeted for frequent stop and search by police officers. They may channel their anger and hostility into subcultural responses such as territorial street gangs.

Tony Sewell – triple quandary theory

Sewell identifies three risk factors that he believes are responsible for high levels of crime committed by African-Caribbean boys.

1. Many African-Caribbean boys are brought up in single-parent families. The absence of fathers means that they lack positive male role models.
2. They feel that they cannot relate to mainstream culture because they believe, for example, that teachers, police officers and employers are racist and therefore working against their interests.
3. They are very influenced by the media's emphasis on **conspicuous consumption** – the idea that identity and status are dependent on material things such as designer labels and jewellery.

Sewell argues that these three quandaries create anxiety for black boys, which is resolved by constructing subcultures or gangs. These gangs become the arena in which young black males gain respect and status from their peers by engaging in hyper-masculine activity such as violence, as well as conspicuous consumption from the proceeds of crime.

Essential notes

Sewell takes a multi-dimensional approach to black street crime. He argues that society needs to take some responsibility for racism and for exaggerating material needs through the media. However, he is also regarded as controversial, because he believes that black people need to take more responsibility for their actions.

Statistical evidence is not routinely collected on the class background of offenders in the UK. However, a range of data sources suggest that most people convicted of indictable (serious) offences, especially those who are imprisoned, tend to be from lower social-class backgrounds. For example, Roger Houchin (2005) found that there was a strong relationship between living in the most deprived wards in Scotland and being in prison. The imprisonment rate in the 27 most deprived wards was around quadruple what it was in Scotland as a whole. In Glasgow, no less than 60% of prisoners came from the most deprived council estates.

Omolade carried out a study of 2171 adult prisoners imprisoned in England and Wales in 2006 and 2007 and found that 43% had no educational qualifications and only 6% had a degree or equivalent. 36% had been unemployed when sentenced, whilst 60% had been claiming benefits. An earlier study carried out by the Prison Reform Working Group (PRWG), which looked at the entire prison population of England and Wales, found that 67% were unemployed prior to imprisonment compared to just 5% in the population as a whole; 32% were homeless (compared with 0.9% of the whole population); whilst 27% had been brought up in care (as opposed to 2% of the whole population).

Similarly, Reiner (2007) points out that 74% of the prison population is drawn from the poorest 20% of the population. Most prisoners prior to their conviction were either unemployed or employed in semi-skilled or unskilled manual work. Hagell and Newburn's study of youth detention centres also found that the vast majority of young offenders came from working-class backgrounds. In contrast, they found that only 8% of persistent offenders came from middle-class homes.

However, these statistics may not give sociologists a truly valid picture of the relationship between class and crime, because:

(a) They only include only those who have been convicted and imprisoned.
(b) Unemployment and claiming benefits may not be accurate measurement of working-class status.
(c) Some crimes which are more likely to be conducted by the middle class, for example, (white-collar crime) are less likely to lead to convictions and imprisonment than crimes which are probably more typically working class (particularly street crimes like burglary, robbery and assault).
(d) **Corporate crimes** are only likely to involve those in senior positions in corporations, while state crime mainly involves those in senior positions in government, and again there may be low recording, conviction and imprisonment rates for these types of crime,
(e) Social class overlaps with other statuses; for example, it is clear that people from ethnic minority backgrounds are over-represented in terms of stops, searches, arrests, convictions and as part of the prison population. It is highly likely that ethnic minorities share aspects of working-class identity – such as poverty, few educational qualifications, social housing and so on – with white working-class people.

Key reasons why the working class people commit more crime

There are a number of sociological theories covered earlier in this book that offer explanations for why working-class people might commit crime, including:

(a) **Functionalist strain theory** (Robert Merton): working-class individuals cannot achieve cultural goals by legitimate means and so turn to crime to attain the goal of material success (see pp 6–7).

(b) **Subcultural strain theory** (Albert Cohen): working-class individuals experience status frustration and turn to crime in order to obtain status from their peers (see p 8).

(c) **Marxism** (David Gordon): the working class are driven to crime as a consequence of criminogenic capitalism and the inequalities/deprivations associated with it. They commit crime in order to survive (see p 10).

(d) **Marxism** (Box): the law is deliberately constructed by the ruling class to discriminate against the working class and to criminalize them and to ensure that ruling-class crimes (white-collar, corporate, green and state crimes), are both under-policed and rarely punished (see p 10).

(e) **Neo-Marxism** (the 'New Criminology'): working-class people are more likely to be alienated in a capitalist society and to choose to protest by committing crimes to vent their frustration (see pp 14–15).

(f) **Labelling theory**: the working class are labelled as potentially criminal by agents of social control and are targeted by the police and punished more severely by the courts. Also, the working class are less likely to negotiate their way out of trouble (see pp 16–18).

(g) **Right Realism** (Charles Murray): most crime is committed by the underclass and their children (see p 20).

(h) **Right Realism** control theory (Travis Hirschi): working-class people have fewer social controls in their lives and consequently the costs to them of committing crime are lower than middle-class people (see p 21).

(i) **Left Realism:** the working class commit crime because of relative deprivation and marginalization (see pp 24–25).

Examiners' notes

There are many theories of crime which are focused on class. For example, there are nine listed on this page. It is recommended that you learn 4 or 5 of these.

Essential notes

There are other sources of data about crime. For example, some sociologists look at court conviction rates for indictable (serious) crimes; others look at prison population statistics. However, interpretivist sociologists suggest that all statistics are socially constructed and may not be **representative** of criminals in general, instead they may tell us more about the institutional biases of the criminal justice system.

Examiners' notes

All the factors – age, gender, ethnicity, locality and social class – may prompt essay questions that require you to explain why certain groups seem to commit more crime than others. Be aware that you can combine some of these factors. For example, female criminality is more likely to be committed by working-class girls, whereas most black teenagers who commit crime in inner-city areas come from deprived backgrounds.

The official crime statistics

Patterns of crime and deviance by ethnicity, gender and social class are outlined in Chapter 1. Much of the information British sociologists get about patterns and trends in crime come from the official crime statistics (OCS). Published quarterly by the government, these are based on:

- crimes reported by victims and the general public, and recorded by the police
- crimes detected and 'cleared up', or solved, by the police
- crimes reported to the **Crime Survey of England and Wales (CSEW)**. The CSEW introduced in 1983, is an annual **survey** of crime victimization, in which about 47,000 adults aged 16 or over and living in private households in England and Wales are interviewed face-to-face about their experiences as victims of property crimes such as burglary, and personal crimes such as assault.

The CSEW is thought to provide a more realistic picture of household and personal crime than the OCS, because it includes crimes that are not reported to the police or recorded by them.

The OCS are used to establish trends and patterns in criminal activity, especially to do with:

- the volume of crime – how much of it there is and whether it is increasing or decreasing: since 2002, overall crime has risen only slightly in the UK; for example, in 2002 there there were nearly 6 million recorded crimes, compared with 6.5 million in 2015 – a rise of about 7%
- the main types of crime – whether or not it takes the form of violence against the person or is property-orientated: property-orientated crimes such as burglary, robbery and theft have steeply declined from 4.9 million in 1994 to 2.9 million in 2015, although violent crimes have increased from 218,000 in 1994 to just over 1 million recorded incidents in 2015; there was also a 14% rise in recorded rapes and other sexual offences between 2015 and 2016
- the 'typical' social characteristics of the people who are reported, arrested and convicted of the crime: the OCS suggest that the 'typical' criminal is likely to be young, male, working class, and possibly from an an ethnic minority background.

Key problems associated with crime statistics

Some sociologists, mainly **positivists**, accept the **validity** of the OCS without question, believing them to be a realistic or truthful picture of crime in the UK. Hence, they have constructed sociological theories to explain why particular social groups appear to commit more crime according to these statistics.

However, others have identified four sets of problems with the official criminal statistics:

1. administrative problems associated with the way crimes are counted
2. problems with victims and their confidence or lack of it in reporting crimes
3. problems with the Crime Survey of England and Wales
4. theoretical problems – particular sociological theories, especially interpretivism as represented by labelling theory, as well as Marxism and feminism, claim the OCS do not provide a reliable or valid picture of crime.

Examiners' notes

It is important to use mass media sources to keep up-to-date with trends in crime. The official statistics are reported and commented on at least twice a year in the newspapers. You should note any interesting patterns and trends to show the examiners that you are aware of contemporary issues.

Administrative problems

1. During 1998–99, the counting rules for crime used by the police changed significantly. In 2002 the National Crime Recording Standard (NCRS) was introduced, which resulted in the introduction of a glut of new offences, such as harassment (stalking), hate crimes (against ethnic minorities, religions and gay people) and violence against police officers whilst resisting arrest. As a result, it is not possible to compare post-2002 official violence statistics with pre-2002 statistics because official definitions of violence have changed.

2. Changes to recording procedures have continued throughout the 21st century. For example, the police now distinguish between violence that results in injury and violence that results in no harm or injury. Police forces are now more likely to record all instances of domestic violence reported to them, however trivial. Online crime, too, is now more consistently recorded.

3. Moreover, the government contributes to these administrative problems by continually introducing new laws, and therefore new crimes. For example, it is estimated that the Labour government of 1997–2010 introduced over 3000 new laws.

4. Historical crime also distorts the validity of the crime statistics; this is crime committed in the past which may only have just come to public or official attention. For example, the 2015 murder statistics jumped 20% compared with 2014 because the official inquest into the deaths of 96 Liverpool football fans in 2015 resulted in 'unlawful death' verdicts which were added to the 2015 murder statistics despite the fact that the deaths had occurred in 1989. The official enquiries into the murders committed by Dr. Harold Shipman and the sexual offences of Jimmy Savile (Operation Yewtree) have led to historical cases, undermining the validity of contemporary murder and sexual offences statistics by artificially inflating them.

5. Pilkington is critical of the OCS because many crimes are not included in them – consequently there exists a **'dark figure'** (or hidden iceberg) of unrecorded crime. For example, some offences are not included in the OCS because they are dealt with by civil agencies such as the HM Revenue and Customs or the Health and Safety Executive rather than by the police or courts, such as tax and VAT fraud committed by companies or wealthy individuals or Health and Safety infringements by employers that result in the death of employees.

6. Self-reports – a type of questionnaire which asks people whether they have committed particular crimes for which they have not been caught or punished – also suggest there is more crime than police recorded crimes indicate. For example, Campbell found that female offending is probably much higher than the OCS indicate, after conducting self-report studies on teenage girls.

The effect of victim reporting on the reliability and validity of the OCS

Victims are central to the OCS. However, they are generally an unreliable source of information about crime because they do not behave in predictable ways. Consequently there is a dark figure of unreported crimes. For example:

- Some institutional victims of crime choose not to report crime. Public and state schools, professional associations such as the British Medical Association (BMA) and the Law Society, and financial institutions such as banks, prefer not to involve the police and courts because of the bad publicity that may be generated for their institutions. For example, schools may expel or suspend students for criminal activity such as vandalism and drugs, rather than involve the police.
- There is evidence from victim surveys that many people, especially working-class people and ethnic minorities living in inner-city areas, do not report crimes against them because of poor police–community relationships. Such groups lack confidence in the police and do not trust them to take their complaints seriously. It is believed that hate crimes such as racist name-calling and vandalism are seriously under-reported for this reason.
- Some victims may not be aware that a crime has been committed against them, for example, children may not understand that they are victims of abuse, while elderly people may not realize they have been defrauded by cowboy builders.
- Some victims, particularly of sex crimes such as rape, may fear humiliation at the hands of the police, the courts, the media and society in general, and so might be reluctant to report this crime against them to the authorities. Rape, in particular, is thought to be greatly under-estimated by the OCS because of this.
- Some crimes are victimless because they involve buying and selling an illegal service (for example, sex) or goods (for example, drugs). Neither party has a vested interest in reporting the crime.
- Criminologists argue that a rise in crime may simply reflect a rise in reporting. For example, property crime may be reported because a police report is required in order to make an insurance claim. When Childline was set up in 1986, the reporting of child abuse increased because children felt more confident that their complaints would be taken seriously. Consequently criminologists have to distinguish between a real increase in crime and an increase in the reporting of crime, which is quite different.

Essential notes

Most criminologists regard the statistics for sexual offences as an unreliable indicator of the real level of sex offences in the UK. For example, between 2010 and 2012, it is estimated that 78,000 people were raped in the UK (69,000 women and 9000 men). However, only 15,670 (approximately 20%) of these rapes were reported to the police. About 80% of rape victims are not reporting the crime against them, because of the police practice of 'no-criming' (that is, the police do not record a high proportion of rapes reported to them because they do not regard the victim as 'reliable') and the very low conviction rates associated with rape (which in the UK hovers between 5% and 6% of accused rapists). Using the internet, research the trial of the footballer Ched Evans, who was accused of rape, and work out why feminists like Sue Lees fear that his acquittal will stop women reporting rape.

👉 **This topic continues on the next four pages**

Problems with the Crime Survey of England and Wales

The Crime Survey of England and Wales (CSEW) is a face-to-face survey of crime, which is used by the Home Office in conjunction with police recorded statistics to work out levels of crime in the UK. The 2015 survey conducted over 35,000 face-to-face structured interviews with a sample of people aged 16 and over living in private households in England and Wales about their experiences of crime in the 12 months prior to the interview. The CSEW is used because it is seen to have several advantages over police recorded crime.

- It uses a large nationally representative sample survey that provides a good measure of long-term crime trends for the offences and the population it covers (that is, those resident in households).
- It covers crimes not reported to the police and is not affected by any changes in police recording practice; it is therefore regarded as a reliable measure of long-term trends.
- The **research population** was extended in 2009 to include children aged 10 to 15.
- A new question asked in 2015 found that cyber-related crime is vastly under-reported.

Recent CSEW findings suggest that about 20% of the population experiences being a victim of crime over the course of a year. Most people are most likely to be victims of vandalism, followed by vehicle-related theft, household theft, and assault. The 2011–12 CSEW shows that there were 2.1 million violent incidents in England and Wales, with 3% of adults victimized. However, the CSEW clearly shows that the number of violent incidents has halved from its peak in 1995, when the survey estimated over 4.2 million violent incidents. Moreover, half of the violent crime reported to the CSEW involved no injury. The CSEW also clearly shows that young men aged 16 to 24 are most at risk of being victims of crime and twice more likely than young women to be victims of crime. Moreover, the CSEW found that the older a person gets, the less likely they are to be a victim of crime. African-Caribbean people reported that they are most frequently victims of street robbery and hate crimes. The CSEW found that poorer households (21%) are 6% more likely to be burgled than higher-income households (15%). Finally, the CSEW concludes that an average person's chances of being a victim of crime are extremely low.

However, sociologists argue that the CSEW may not be a reliable indicator of crime for the following reasons:

- The survey does not cover commercial victimization, such as thefts from businesses and shops or frauds.
- It excludes victimless crimes (such as possession of drugs and prostitution). Questions have been asked about people's drug use, but asking people to self-report their own crimes is not thought to be reliable.

- Groups such as the unemployed and homeless are under-represented by the CSEW.
- The CSEW relies on victims having objective knowledge of the crimes committed against them. However, people's memories with regard to traumatic events are often unreliable; there is a danger of **subjective** exaggeration as well as the telescoping of incidents (i.e. people unconsciously move them forward and backward in time).
- People may be unaware that they have been victims – especially if they are children or the elderly. Consequently, they cannot report the crime to the CSEW.
- Pilkington questions the objectivity of the CSEW, because he argues that the main function of the survey is to reassure the general public that the likelihood of being a victim of crime in the UK is very slight.
- Left Realists John Lea and Jock Young, who conducted the Islington Crime Survey, criticize government victim surveys for focusing on the wrong samples of the population. They argue that victim surveys need to focus on inner-city areas. They found that poorer people who lived in deprived areas were frequent victims of street crimes. The effect of crimes such as burglary were particularly hard on the poor, because they could neither afford insurance nor afford to design crime out of their lives by investing in alarms and cameras. The CSEW tell us very little about the day-to-day experience of living in high-crime areas. The residents of these areas have a well-above-average chance of being a victim of crime.

Theoretical problems with the official crime statistics

It is often assumed that the official crime statistics (OCS) are **reliable** and valid in the picture of crime and criminality that they present. However, interpretivist sociologists (see p 32) argue that the OCS are of limited usefulness because they are a **social construction.** This means that the statistics may tell us more about the decisions of the social groups involved in their collection – particularly the police and the courts – than they tell us about crime and criminals.

A type of interpretivist theory – labelling theory (also known as interactionism) argues that the OCS tell us more about the nature of **policing** in the UK than about crime and criminality. In particular, the OCS may tell us a great deal about how police officers interact with suspects, especially those from relatively powerless social groups. Therefore, interpretivists question the validity of the picture of criminality that the OCS provides. They suggest that young, working-class and African-Caribbean people frequently appear in these statistics because they are

☞ This topic continues on the next two pages

Essential notes

The police may exercise discretion in terms of how they define and consequently count crime, because of political pressures to improve their clear-up rates or to improve efficiency. Crimes may be redefined by the police as 'less serious', for example, attempted burglary. Car theft may be defined as 'criminal damage'. Some crimes may not be recorded because the police regard them as too trivial to classify.

Essential notes

It is important not to dismiss all police officers as racist. Most sociologists accept that a minimal number of police officers are prejudiced against ethnic minorities. The MacPherson Report suggests that institutional racism – a form of unwitting prejudice, ignorance, thoughtlessness and racial stereotyping, which disadvantages minority ethnic groups – is a greater problem than individual police officers acting in racist ways. This type of racism is not deliberate; it is ingrained in outdated organizational policies and ways of dealing with people.

profiled and targeted by the police rather than because they are more criminal. This can be illustrated in several ways:

- Separate studies of police officers on patrol conducted by D. J. Smith and J. Grey in the UK and Aaron Cicourel in the USA indicate that they operate using stereotypical assumptions or labels about what constitutes 'suspicious' or 'criminal' behaviour; that is, the police decision to stop or arrest someone may be based on whether they correspond to a stereotype.
- Criminologists have estimated that, for every 100 crimes committed, 47 will be reported to the police, 27 will be recorded by the police and 5 will be cleared up in the form of a caution or conviction.
- **Self-report studies** indicate that the volume of crime should be greater and that females and middle-class males are just as likely to commit a crime as those included in the crime statistics.
- There is strong sociological evidence that suggests racial profiling by some police officers may be a crucial element governing their decision to stop African-Caribbeans. Bowling and Phillips noted that some police officers in London based their decision to stop young black males in cars on a stereotype known as 'driving while black'. Police officers assumed that black youths were driving upmarket cars because either they were drug dealers or they had stolen them.
- Feminist criminologists argue that male officers tend to adopt paternalistic attitudes towards female offenders, who are less likely to be stopped, arrested and charged. For example, when caught committing criminal offences, they are more likely to be cautioned than arrested and charged. Pollack calls this the **chivalry factor**, 49% of female offenders received a caution. Only 30% of male offenders received the same. Research also indicates that police culture is very masculine (fewer than 20% of police officers are women) and interaction with men or ethnic minorities may be shaped by a need to be seen by other officers as tough.

The Marxist critique of the OCS

Marxists are also very critical of the OCS. They suggest that the capitalist state collects and constructs criminal statistics in order to serve the interests of the ruling class. The statistics serve an ideological function – whoever has the power to collect and construct such statistics has the power to control and manipulate public opinion. Therefore, Marxists argue that the ideological function of the OCS is to criminalize groups such as the young, the working class and African-Caribbeans. This divides and rules the working class and diverts white conformist working-class attention away from class inequalities.

Furthermore, Steven Box argues that the OCS also diverts attention from both middle-class white-collar and **corporate crime**. Box argues that crimes committed by the powerful are not pursued as vigorously or punished as harshly as working-class crimes. He also argues that the powerful engage in anti-social activities which result in death, injury and theft for ordinary people but are often not defined as criminal because the ruling class constructs laws to reflect their own interests.

Finally, Left Realists such as Jock Young and John Lea (see pp 24–25) note that the Islington Crime Survey data suggest that the OCS are largely correct and that young working-class people and, depending on the area, African-Caribbean people do commit more crime than other social groups, despite the influence of moral panics, police stereotyping and judicial bias.

Examiners' notes

Note that you can raise all these points when answering essay questions requiring you to explain why particular social groups such as ethnic minorities are more likely to appear criminal.

Examiners' notes

It is important to group arguments for and against the OCS into theoretical categories. Most arguments in favour of the use of statistics are positivist. Interpretivists are generally critical of the ways in which statistics are collected. However, do not neglect the Marxist position, as it gives insight into why few middle-class crimes are included in the official picture of crime.

News does not just happen – it is a socially manufactured product. This means that it is the end result of a complex process involving journalists and editors applying a set of criteria known as **news values** to judge if a story is newsworthy, or whether it will attract an audience.

Crime is newsworthy because bad news, rather than good news, attracts audiences. Violent and sexual crimes are generally viewed as more newsworthy than property crime, as these crimes are more easily personalized and usually more dramatic. Crimes such as murder, kidnap and stranger rape are newsworthy because they are relatively rare. Crime is often reported as a human interest story, in the sense that it could happen to anyone.

However, such news values can result in crime reporting not representing the true reality of crime. Jason Ditton and James Duffy found that 46% of media reports were about violent or sexual crimes, although these types of crimes only made up 3% of crimes recorded by the police. There is also evidence of increasing media preoccupation with sex crimes. Keith Soothill and Sylvia Walby (1991) found that newspaper reporting of rape cases increased from under one-quarter of all cases in 1951 to over one-third in 1985.

Key study

Felson and media fallacies about crime

Richard Felson argues that media reporting reinforces certain fallacies or falsehoods about crime:

- Age fallacy – media representations give the impression that all age groups are involved in crime
- Class fallacy – the media suggest that the middle class are most likely to be crime victims. However this is untrue. The poor are much more likely to be the victims of crime.
- Ingenuity fallacy – the media convey that criminals are clever, yet most crime is opportunistic – done on the spur of the moment
- Police fallacy – the media may give the impression that the police are more efficient than they really are
- Dramatic fallacy – the media focus only on the most violent crimes, thus creating fear of crime; media reporting may encourage fear of crime, especially among the elderly and women, by over-focusing on crimes against these groups.

The media as a possible cause of crime

There has long been concern that media content has a negative effect on the behaviour of young people, especially children. Television, films, comics, music lyrics (especially rap), the internet and computer games have all been accused of causing violence and anti-social behaviour.

There are seven main areas of concern:

1. The media is portrayed as a powerful secondary agent of socialization, which shapes the behaviour of young people. For example, it has been argued that young impressionable audiences often imitate the violent, immoral or anti-social behaviour seen on television or in the cinema and this produces a copycat effect in terms of crime and delinquency.

2. It is argued that frequent violence onscreen persuades children that violence is a legitimate way to solve their problems.
3. The media is often accused of **desensitizing** children and teenagers to the effects of violence for its victims by exposing children to a constant diet of violence in films and on television.
4. Some say the media encourage crime and deviance by glamorizing crime and criminals and exposing children to deviant role models.
5. The media have been accused of transmitting knowledge of criminal techniques such as drug-taking.
6. The media have been accused of portraying the police as incompetent.
7. The media and advertisers have been accused by Left Realists, Marxists and **neo-functionalists**, e.g. Reiner, of promoting individualism, greed and self-interest and thus increasing feelings of relative deprivation, resentment and envy among the 'have-nots' section of the population. Sociologists such as Reiner argue these feelings may motivate the 'have-not' sector of the population to commit crime.

Thousands of sociological and psychological research studies have looked into possible links between media content and crime. However, most sociologists note that this link is too simplistic, as it fails to see that audiences differ in terms of factors such as age, social class, intelligence and level of education, so they do not react in the same way to media content. The argument also fails to appreciate the nature of violence – most experts say it is caused by a complex range of factors: poor socialization, bad parenting, peer group influences, mental illness, drugs or alcohol.

Key study

David Morrison – the effect of violence on audiences

David Morrison showed a range of violent film clips to groups of women, young men and war veterans. All groups thought a very violent scene from *Pulp Fiction* was humorous, due to its light-hearted dialogue.

However, a scene from *Ladybird, Ladybird* showing domestic violence caused distress for all three groups due to the realism of the setting, the perceived unfairness and because child actors were part of the scene. Morrison concludes that the context in which violence on screen takes place affects its impact on the audience.

Richard Sparks notes that many media effects studies ignore the meanings that viewers give to media violence. There is evidence that audiences interpret violence in cartoons, horror films and news quite differently. For example, David Buckingham's research suggests that even very young children are **media literate** and use the media in a responsible way.

Guy Cumberbatch reviewed over 3500 studies on the relationship between the media and violence and failed to find one that proved the connection. None disproved it either. As he concludes, 'the jury is still out on this issue'.

Essential notes

Think about the relationship between media representations of crime, gender and fear of crime. Research a week's selection of TV programmes to see how often women appear as victims of violence, and compare it with what victim surveys say about women's chances of being victims of crime.

Essential notes

It is worth researching aspects of this debate so that you can illustrate these arguments and/ or their criticisms. Many people believe that the murder of the toddler Jamie Bulger in Liverpool in 1993 by two other children was connected to their viewing of the horror movie 'Childs Play 3'. You should research this case to investigate whether the police, judge or sociologists made this connection. However you should also update and make current the debate by researching the role of social media in the London riots of 2011.

☞ **This topic continues on the next two pages**

Moral panics

Moral panic theory originates in interactionist theory. A moral panic refers to intense public concern or anxiety about a social problem or social group that has been brought to public attention by the mass media, especially the tabloid newspapers. The moral panic usually amplifies the threat of the problem or group out of all proportion to its real seriousness.

Key study

Stan Cohen: Folk devils and moral panics

The terms 'folk devil' and 'moral panic' were first used by Stan Cohen in his analysis of the social reaction to various incidents involving mods and rockers at UK coastal resorts in 1964.

Moral panics usually go through the following stages:

- The media report a particular event or group in a negative and stereotypical way, using sensationalist, emotional and exaggerated headlines and language.
- Follow-up articles engage in the **demonization** of the group and consequently construct the group as folk devils.
- The media engage in **symbolization** – focusing on the group's symbols (e.g. dress, hairstyles and music), which it associates with trouble and violence, so the group becomes visible to the general public.
- The media invites people with influence – **moral entrepreneurs**, e.g. politicians, experts, bishops – to condemn the group/behaviour.
- The media predicts further trouble from the group.
- This puts pressure on the authorities – politicians, police and courts – to curb the problem group and activity, and so control it. At this stage, more policing and severe judicial punishments often occur.
- A **self-fulfilling prophecy** develops as the group resists the attempts to control it or acts up to the media, which leads to arrests and a spiral of further negative reporting.

Moral panic theorists such as Cohen, and Jock Young, note that moral panics often result in **deviancy amplification** – the media reaction worsens the problem they initially set out to condemn. What was initially a fantasy problem becomes a very real problem.

Why moral panics occur

Three main theories purport to explain why moral panics occur:

- Moral panics seem to arise most often when society is undergoing a 'moral crisis'. Such crises are usually linked to major social change or modernization; for example, the first moral panics about youth in the 1950s and 1960s coincided with youth becoming a consumer group in its own right, with its own very distinctive values and norms, often viewed as immoral and threatening by the older generation. Cohen suggested that the emergence of youth cultures was seen by the older generation as undermining both the moral order and traditional authority.

- It is said they are deliberately created by journalists to sell newspapers by tapping into the fears of readers. Moral panics tend to stimulate circulation and thus the profits of media companies.
- Marxists such as Stuart Hall suggest that the capitalist state uses moral panics to divert attention from the mismanagement of capitalism, especially wealth and income inequalities see pp 14–15.

Evaluation of moral panic theory

- John Muncie notes that, like labelling theory, moral panic theory has drawn our attention to the role and power of the media in defining normal and deviant behaviour. It has given us some sociological insight into the consequences of labelling in terms of how labelled groups react to media demonization. The moral panic thesis also reminds us to continually question our commonsensical understanding of crime and especially the media reporting of crime.
- Some commentators claim that moral panics do not reflect social or moral anxieties held by the majority of society's members – rather, they are quite simply the product of the desire of journalists and editors to sell newspapers. They are a good example of how audiences are manipulated by the media for commercial purposes.
- Left Realists argue that moral panics are often based on reality or fact – the groups identified are often a very real threat to those living in inner-city areas. Left Realists, however, note that moral panic theorists often deny the reality of the subject matter of moral panics and portray them as fantasies made up by journalists. Young and John Lea note that portraying such crime as a fantasy product of the mass media is naive because such crime has real negative outcomes for people living in inner-city areas.
- Angela McRobbie and Sarah Thornton argue that the concept of moral panic is now outdated in this era of sophisticated media technology and 24-hour rolling news. Most events are no longer reported for long enough to sustain the interest that traditional moral panics generated in the past. However recent analysis of social networking sites suggest that Twitter can initiate and even accelerate moral panics as can false news stories on Facebook.

Examiners' notes

Questions on moral panics can appear in their own right, so it is important that you have a developed knowledge of this social phenomenon. However, if a more general question on the relationship between crime and media should appear, you will need to balance moral panics alongside other aspects of media coverage of crime and the idea that the mass media might be partially responsible for increases in particular types of crime.

Examiners' notes

Be aware that a question on the relationship between the media and crime can be daunting, in that there is a lot of ground to cover. You will not be able to include everything in the limited time available, so you must decide what to include and what to leave out. However, do try to include the moral panic theory.

Essential notes

The work of the journalist Misha Glenny is essential to our understanding of global crime. It is strongly recommended that you either watch his TED Talk on organized global crime or read his very entertaining books McMafia; Seriously Organized Crime and 'Dark Crime: Cybercops and You'.

Essential notes

Not all criminologists agree on how to define global crime. For example, 2010 saw the emergence of the website WikiLeaks, which released hundreds of thousands of confidential US cables from American embassies around the world on a range of sensitive political issues. The US government views Julian Assange, who founded the site, as a criminal, whereas others see him as a crusader for democracy.

Globalization refers to the increasing interconnectedness of societies, so that what happens in one locality is shaped by distant events in another, and vice versa. It is caused by the spread of new information and media technologies, especially the internet and satellite television, cheap air travel, mass tourism, mass migration, and the increase in the number of **transnational corporations** that produce and market their goods and brands in a global marketplace.

Just as there is a legitimate global capitalist economy, so there is also an illegitimate or criminal global economy, which Manuel Castells argues is worth over £1 trillion a year. Glenny (2009) refers to global organized crime as the 'global shadow economy' and estimates that it accounts for about 15% of the world's gross national production (GDP). He argues that the success of global organized crime is 'one of the great, albeit largely unknown, commercial success stories of the past 20 years, comparable, in its own very peculiar way, to the achievements of Microsoft or Google'. This global criminal economy has a number of features mirroring the global capitalist economy. Glenny observes that organized crime in a globalizing world operates in the same way as any other business:

- It has zones of production, like Afghanistan and Colombia, which, for example, are involved in the production of cocaine and heroin respectively.
- It has zones of distribution, like Mexico, Jamaica and the Balkans, in which organized gangs control the movement of: cocaine into the USA and, in the case of Jamaica, Europe; and, in the case of the Balkans, women trafficked for prostitution into the UK, Germany and Scandinavia.
- It has zones of consumption, like the European Union, Japan and the USA. Many global criminal networks have developed to feed a demand from the affluent West for drugs and prostitution.

Glenny also points out that the zones of production and distribution are mainly found in the developing world and are often characterized by 'appalling violence and bloodshed'. For instance, Glenny notes that about 1000 people a year are killed in Mexico as a direct result of the war between organized gangs to control the distribution of cocaine into the USA. He also observes that, since 1998, five million people have died as a result of a civil war in the Democratic Republic of Congo, which local paramilitaries have sought to sell raw materials such as coltan (a rare metal used in mobile phones) and diamonds to organized criminals in return for weapons.

D. Hobbs and C. Dunningham observe that global criminal networks often serve and feed off established local or domestic criminal networks. They note that crime is increasingly 'glocal' in character, meaning that it is still locally based but is now more likely to have global connections. Examples of 'glocal' trade are:

- The illegal drugs trade, worth £300–£400 billion annually. Local prices and the availability of drugs in any city in the UK depend on how efficiently global gangs can move drugs around the world while avoiding detection. Moreover, a great deal of crime in British cities such as street robbery, shoplifting and burglary is fuelled by the need to finance a heroin or crack habit. It is estimated by Drugwise that there may be 306,000 heroin users in the UK.
- Sex trafficking for prostitution – for example, it is estimated that between 3000 and 4000 women have been trafficked into the UK by organized Eastern European gang to work as constrained prostitutes.
- Smuggling legal goods such as alcohol, tobacco and cars. Glenny estimates that the UK loses about £6 billion a year in taxes from cigarettes smuggled into Britain from Eastern Europe.
- Counterfeiting designer goods and labels.

New global communications have created fresh opportunities for crime. The internet has generated new types of global fraud known as **cyber crime**. The UK government estimates that the annual cost of cyber attacks for British companies is £27 billion per annum. These new cyber crimes involve:

- Identity theft – cyber criminals obtain personal data from individuals (such as address, date of birth or bank account details) and exploit this online by opening bogus accounts (for example, bank accounts and mortgage applications). In many cases, the victims of identity theft are not even aware of a problem until the impacts become severe.
- Fraud – in November 2016, a cyber attack on the Tesco bank resulted in over 20,000 customers having money stolen from their accounts.
- Online scams – cyber criminals obtain financial or other valuable information by fraudulent means.

Examiners' notes

Evaluative thinking is important. For example, think about how difficult it is to research activities that are carried out by dangerous powerful individuals and groups in secrecy. The task is even more difficult, because not all sociologists agree on what is 'criminal'.

☞ This topic continues on the next two pages

Essential notes

Anonymous is perhaps the most notorious of all hacker groups. It is a decentralized online community of tens of thousands of anonymous 'hacktivists', who use their combined computer skills to attack and bring down websites as a form of political protest. The group became known for a series of attacks on government, religious, and corporate websites. It has attacked the Pentagon, threated to take down Facebook, threatened, the Mexican drug cartel and declared war on Scientology. It also publicly supported the Occupy Wall Street movement in 2011, attacking the website of the New York Stock Exchange.

Examiners' notes

Another way to evaluate is simply to explore the way crime has evolved because of globalization.

- Money laundering – cyber criminals use online means to launder the proceeds of criminal acts (for example, through complex, internet-enabled transfers between global or offshore bank accounts).
- IP theft – cyber criminals, often sponsored by rival organizations or nation states, steal ideas, designs, product specifications, trade secrets, process information or methodologies, which can greatly erode competitive advantage or even the operational or technological advantage prized by nation states over potential adversaries.

The UK government has identified four types of groups that are responsible for the majority of cyber crime in the UK:

1. Organized criminal networks. These are supposedly focusing more of their attention on cyber crime because it offers attractive rewards for minimal investment and low risk.
2. Foreign intelligence services that may sponsor or engage directly in widespread industrial espionage.
3. Terrorist organizations such as ISIS may attempt to hack into aspects of British infrastructure such as air-traffic control in order to bring down aircraft or power grids to cause widespread disruption and fear.
4. Hacker groups such as Anonymous, Lizard Squad and DDoS engage in 'hacktivism', meaning they gain unauthorized access to computer files or networks in order to further social or political goals.

Taylor argues that globalization has made it easier for elite groups and transnational corporations to move funds and profits around the world to avoid taxation. There may also be overlap between criminal organizations and the powerful wealthy elites who run the legitimate capitalist global economy, as the former invest in 'legitimate' businesses in an attempt to launder profits from crime. Glenny also notes that offshore banking has advantaged global criminals because it has made it easier for gangs to launder cash from their illegal activities through mainstream banks in tax havens. Glenny notes that banks like Barclays and Nat West have been too happy to accept deposits from very dubious sources without questions being asked. In 2012, HSBC admitted laundering hundreds of millions of dollars for the world's biggest crime syndicate, the Mexican Sinaloa narco cartel. The bank was fined $2 billion by the US Department of Justice. In 2015, the Financial Conduct Authority fined Barclays Bank £72 million for failing to run sufficient checks on deposits that might have been attempting to launder drug money or to finance terrorism.

Global crime is difficult to police, because international laws are ill defined and international criminal justice agencies do not have the global powers to pursue global criminals. Cooperation between international agencies is limited, or hindered by conflict between local and international police agencies, and also conflict between governments.

Marxist criminologists such as Stephen Box point out that many global crimes are committed by powerful people, who use their influence to ensure that no laws exist to criminalize their activities, and consequently they face little risk of punishment. This has led to some radical criminologists arguing that 'crime' needs to be redefined – rather than meaning 'activities that break domestic or international laws', crimes need to include all activities that harm living species and the environment in which they live. The idea of studying such harms is known as **zemiology**.

Essential notes

Think about how cyber crime fits into Ulrich Beck's theory of society, which suggests that industrial societies have entered a phase he calls 'second modernity'. He argues this phase is characterized by globalization. Moreover, societies in this phase are risk societies. This is because science and technology bring benefits but they also bring about the possibility or risk of harm. Beck argues that the main role of states in the period of second modernity is the management of risks such as cyber crime and terrorist attacks, which might utilize sophisticated technology, for example, 'dirty' bombs.

Green crime refers to crime against the environment. Green crime is increasingly seen as a form of global crime for two reasons:

1. The planet is regarded as a single ecosystem in which human beings, other species and the environment are interconnected and interdependent. Harm done to other species or aspects of the environment, such as the air, water supplies, the ocean and the rainforest, are increasingly seen as impacting negatively on the quality and future of human life wherever it is in the world. For example, radioactive fallout from the Chernobyl nuclear reactor disaster of 1986 spread thousands of miles across Europe, resulting in the banning of sheep farming in parts of England and Wales.

2. Green crime generally tends to be carried out by powerful interests, particularly transnational corporations such as oil and chemical companies working with the cooperation of nation states and local wealthy elites.

Manufactured risks

Ulrich Beck points out that many of the threats to the ecosystem are **manufactured risks** and are the result of the massive demand for consumer goods and the technology that underpins it. Human demand for manufactured goods has potentially negative effects for both humanity and the environment, in that increasing greenhouse gas emissions are contributing to global warming and climate change, and the possibility of future disasters such as flooding. Beck notes that we now live in societies threatened by global risks.

Radical criminologists such as Rob White argue that the present criminal law is inadequate for dealing with green crime. He takes a more radical approach and argues that green crime should be defined as 'any action that harms the physical environment and any of the creatures that live within it, even if no law has been technically broken'. White points out that many of the worst environmental harms committed by big business or the state are not actually illegal and therefore not criminal. Moreover, he argues that current laws are inconsistent in that they often differ across different countries, and are biased in that they are often too influenced by businesses with a vested interest in doing harm to the environment, because their business is the extraction of raw materials or the exploitation of natural environments such as rainforests. White argues that only a green criminology that is focused on the idea of environmental harm can develop a truly global perspective on **green crimes**.

White argues that green criminology takes an **eco-centric view** of environmental harm – it sees such harm as damage to the environment and/or other species of creature, and ultimately to the future of the human race. This view opposes the more **anthropocentric** view of big business, which assumes that humans have the right to exploit the environment and other species for their own benefit. White argues that this capitalist ideology is responsible for a great deal of environmental harm.

Examiners' notes

It is important not to confuse Beck with postmodernist theory. He argues that modern societies have entered a stage of late-modernity rather than a **postmodern** age. Becks's theory is a useful way to evaluate postmodernism.

Examiners' notes

Think about your evaluative approach to this zemiological eco-centric view of green crime. There are problems of interpretation (What counts as 'harm'?) and ideology (who defines what counts as crime?)

Key study

Nigel South – classifying green crimes

Nigel South classifies green crime into primary crimes and secondary crimes.

Primary crimes are the direct result of the destruction and degradation of the planet's resources and include:

- crimes of air pollution such as industrial carbon and greenhouse gas emissions
- crimes of **deforestation** such as illegal logging
- crimes of species decline and animal rights
- crimes of freshwater and marine pollution such as oil spillages.

South identifies secondary green crimes as those which involve flouting existing laws and regulations – for example:

- dumping toxic waste, particularly in the developing world
- breaches of health and safety rules, causing disasters such as Chernobyl and Bhopal
- offloading products such as pharmaceuticals onto Third World markets after they have been banned on safety grounds in the West
- aggression towards environmentalist organisations such as Greenpeace by agents of the State, for example, the blowing up of the Greenpeace ship Rainbow Warrior by the French Secret Service in 1985.

Essential notes

Operationalizing means the measurement of abstract concepts by defining them in research such as by writing questionnaire questions. For example, crime is easy to measure because it is defined legally, but harm is more difficult to define and measure because it is often a matter of interpretation.

Policing green crime

However, green crime is extremely difficult to police for two main reasons:

1. There are very few local or international laws governing the state of the environment. International laws are particularly difficult to construct, because not all countries agree to sign up to global agreements. For example, both China and the USA have been reluctant to agree to meet international targets to reduce carbon emissions.
2. Many of the laws that do exist are shaped by powerful capitalist interests, especially global 'big business'. Governments, especially in the developing world, are generally reluctant to rein in transnational corporations, because they are dependent on the income these companies generate in the form of taxation. Enforcement of laws that do exist to protect the environment is often weak.

Evaluation of green criminology

- Green criminology recognizes the growing importance of environmental issues and manufactured global risks.
- It recognizes the interdependence of humans, other species and the environment.
- However, its focus on harm rather than criminality means that green criminology is often accused of being engaged with subjective interpretation rather than objective scientific analysis, and is therefore biased.

Examiners' notes

It would make sense to use green crime to illustrate the criminogenic nature of capitalism if an exam essay title focuses on Marxist explanations of crime and deviance.

Essential notes

It is very difficult for sociologists to research state crime and therefore to work out its true extent and nature. The dark figure of state crime is probably greater than the dark figure of unreported and unrecorded conventional crime.

Essential notes

Another contemporary example of a possible state crime was the joint USA/UK decision to invade Iraq to remove Saddam Hussein from power. Many commentators point out that this decision broke international laws, because President Bush and Prime Minister Blair had not secured the agreement of the international community via the United Nations Security Council. It is controversially argued that both Bush and Blair are technically war criminals.

Essential notes

It is recommended that you watch the video on YouTube In which Chris Hitchens volunteers to be waterboarded.

State crime is defined as those illegal activities carried out by the agents of the state – such as the armed services, the secret services, civil servants, the police and prison services – on behalf of governments and political leaders in order to further state interests. Such activities are illegal in that they break domestic or international laws.

Most criminologists accept that crimes committed by states across the world would probably include **genocide**, **ethnic cleansing**, the use of torture, assassination of political opponents, supporting terrorist activities against elected governments and invading less powerful states.

Some criminologists have focused on how the state represses its own citizens and have looked at the number of questionable deaths in police custody and suicides in prison, as well as shootings by the police.

Chris Hitchens argued that the USA was guilty of state crimes during its 'war on terror', which abused the human rights of people that the USA suspected of being terrorists. Two types of abuse were identified by Hitchens:

1. Extraordinary rendering – the CIA abducted and illegally transferred suspected Islamists to so-called 'Black-sites' in other countries, which had no laws prohibiting torture.
2. The Bush administration authorized the use of 'enhanced interrogation' or torture at these sites, including waterboarding. The CIA would often use foreign torturers to apply the enhanced interrogation techniques on their behalf.

Eugene McLaughlin has also identified censorship of the media and institutional racism as state crimes. Herman Schwendinger argues that definitions of state crimes should be extended to include human rights crimes. He suggests that any violation of people's human rights should be defined as illegal and therefore criminal. However, Schwendinger's definition of human rights is broad. He suggests that if some groups are denied the same opportunities as the majority population on the basis of racism, sexism and **homophobia**, or if they are economically exploited, then the unequal conditions that result are the result of crimes against human rights.

Disagreement about state crime

There is much disagreement about what constitutes state crime for the following reasons:

- State crime is carried out by powerful people or groups who can define their activities as being legitimate. This makes measuring the extent of state crimes difficult, especially as these activities are often carried out by the most secretive agencies of the state. Governments have the power and resources to cover up such activities and can actually control the flow of information and especially the media by issuing legal instructions to prevent journalists from speaking about state crimes, in the 'public interest'.

- The powerful can impose on society their definition of what counts as crime. What is defined as crime or violence is an ideological construct. Governments have the power to define killing as a problem if it is done by a member of the public, but as justified if done by a police officer or soldier. This ideological relativity can be seen with regard to who the powerful define as terrorists or freedom fighters, and what counts as a 'war crime'. For example, the Holocaust has been defined as a war crime, but dropping the atom bomb on the Japanese cities Hiroshima and Nagasaki was defined by the West as 'necessary'.

- Stan Cohen criticizes Schwendinger's view that state crime should include violations of human rights. Cohen notes that genocide and torture are clearly crimes, but argues that economic exploitation is not clearly criminal, even if it is morally unacceptable. Furthermore, he argues there is not enough agreement about what constitutes 'human rights'. For example, most people accept that freedom should be a human right but not everyone would agree that freedom from poverty is a right.

- Cohen argues that it is difficult to find out the true extent of state crime because governments either deny their actions or attempt to justify their actions in an attempt to cover up their illegal nature. For example, if denial of a massacre does not work, the state will suggest that it was **collateral damage** or that it was necessary to protect national security.

- Cohen notes that perpetrators of crimes on behalf of the state often do not see themselves as criminal. He argues that they use **techniques of neutralization** to deny or justify crimes against people. For example, they deny their victims humanity by labelling them terrorists or extremists. They deny the injury or damage they have done by suggesting that the other side started it, or they deny responsibility by saying they were simply obeying orders or doing their duty. These perpetrators often appeal to a higher cause – for example, the defence of the free world – to legitimize their actions and appear less criminal.

- Herbert Kelman and V. Lee Hamilton also note that many state crimes are actually 'crimes of obedience' – people commit them because they have been socialized into believing it is their duty to obey and that their behaviour is acceptable and necessary (rather than criminal) because the enemy are animals and monsters to which the normal rules of morality do not apply. For example, there is evidence that many members of the Nazi SS justified their action in killing Jews in this way.

- Critics of the concept of 'state crime' argue that the so-called 'criminality' of the act may be outweighed by the fact that the act was committed in the national interest. Some argue that it may be necessary to go beyond the limits of the law in defeating terrorism, so that assassination and torture may be 'necessary evils'.

Strategies for the prevention and control of crime have generally come from two broad sociological sources – Right Realism and Left Realism (see pp 20–25). Both theories are concerned with explaining and preventing those crimes that negatively impact upon the daily lives of ordinary people. However, their focus is often quite different, as described below.

Right Realists	Emphasize the individual. They note that people choose to commit crime because the benefits outweigh the costs. So society needs to look at ways to increase the costs of crime.
Left Realists	Focus on the organization of society, especially the inequality, disadvantage and poverty that result from this, and that create the environment in which crime might be the norm.

Table 4
The focus of Right Realists and of Left Realists

Situational crime prevention

Situational crime prevention (SCP) refers to Right Realist measures aimed at reducing opportunities for crime. It focuses on encouraging potential victims to 'design out' crime by making themselves 'harder targets' by investing in more security and surveillance. The aim is to increase the risk of the criminal being caught and/or deterring criminality by reducing the opportunity for crime.

There is some evidence that car manufacturers' investment in satellite technology, disabling devices and computerized locking systems has reduced the level of car theft in the UK. It is also argued that increased surveillance in shops via CCTV, or security guards and store detectives, increases the likelihood of shoplifters being caught. For other examples of SCP measures and an evaluation of their merits in reducing crime, see pp 56–58.

Surveillance

David Lyon argues that systematic surveillance has become a routine and inescapable part of everyday life in modern times. He argues that societies like the UK, which has one camera for every 11 people in the population, have become surveillance societies, which produce surveillance knowledge which is used to label and categorize individuals and to mark them as a particular type of person. This type of surveillance is top–down centralized surveillance, in that the powerful few, such as the police and security services, scan the masses looking for signs of possible deviance, criminality and delinquency.

The philosopher Jeremy Bentham's concept of the 'panopticon' is useful when discussing the role of surveillance in modern societies. The panopticon was his design for a prison or all-seeing place in which people can be seen wherever they are by observers or guards. Lyon argues that surveillance societies are social panopticons, which induce self-discipline because people are uncertain and fearful about whether they are being watched. Consequently they are more likely to conform to the rules rather than break them.

Foucault argues that surveillance represents a new type of power. He argues that many societies have replaced traditional forms of power, which he calls 'sovereign' power (represented by brutal forms of punishment such as the death penalty and public executions), with 'disciplinary' power (represented by surveillance), because this is a more effective method of deterring deviance and controlling people. For example, Lyon argues that there is evidence that the anxiety associated with not knowing whether they are being watched alters people's behaviour. They consciously avoid acting suspicious and visibly conform to whatever rules govern the situation they are in. However, Foucault sees surveillance as going far beyond CCTV. He believes experts such as doctors, psychiatrists, social workers, teachers are all practitioners of disciplinary power and engaged in surveillance and control and, most importantly, correction of social behaviour.

Evaluating Foucault's concept of the social panopticon model of surveillance

However, there are a number of criticisms of Foucault's concept of disciplinary power and surveillance.

- Firstly, Foucault did not anticipate the convergence of digital technology and data, which Deleuze and Guattari refer to as the 'assemblage of surveillance' activities, which means data is now often assembled from a range of surveillance techniques including DNA, blood type, birth certificate, national insurance and NHS numbers, identity cards, mobile phones and biometric passports, which paint a digital version of particular citizens.
- Secondly, some critics of Foucault suggest that he neglects the surveillance of the powerful by the masses. Mathiesen refers to this as 'synoptic surveillance' or the 'synopticon'. He suggests that the internet, and particularly social media, have undermined traditional and hierarchical top–down surveillance.
- Thirdly, Foucault did not predict that surveillance techniques might be used against the powerful. The popularity of Twitter, blogging and social media sites such as Facebook has transformed surveillance, because these sites can quickly disseminate information to millions of people, which can damage political and professional reputations and careers. For example, UK Uncut uses social media to organize sit-ins, or 'bail-ins', at stores and bank branches of companies that it accuses of avoiding paying tax, such as Vodafone, whilst change. org has used online petitions to push the powerful, across a range of societies, to make social or legal changes which have improved the human rights of vulnerable groups. Groups such as Black Lives Matter may film police behaviour on their mobile phones and upload these to social media sites, therefore creating a situation in which the police become aware of the need to police their own behaviour, especially with regard to their use of violence or illegal stops and detentions. The self-discipline of road users may be encouraged by the increasing number of dashboard cameras in cars or those mounted on cyclists' helmets. People may be less likely to go into 'road rage' mode if they know they might be filmed. Lyon, too, observes that the market for domestic surveillance technologies has dramatically grown as parents buy gadgets such as Day Care cams which permit them to see what their toddlers are up to. Nanny cams monitor for suspected abuse, whilst cameras are increasingly being installed by relatives in the rooms

Essential notes

Surveillance occurs in all areas of life and goes beyond watching or monitoring people or cars via cameras. It involves the processing of all kinds of data, such as the multiple checks at airports, baggage and full-body screening, passport control and ticket checks, the use of supermarket loyalty cards and credit cards which can track what type of consumer you are, the use of internet cookies (which websites use to pass messages to your browser) or the software in mobile phones which means that your location and movements can be tracked.

☞ This topic continues on the next four pages

Examiners' notes

All solutions to crime adopted by governments are social policies. Therefore the material on situational, environmental and Left Realist crime prevention solutions is useful to illustrate any Theory and Method question on the relationship between social policy and sociology.

Examiners' notes

Any essay question on crime in urban areas, or cities, can refer to Wilson's theory (also known as 'broken windows theory') and solutions. It can also be linked to Right Realism.

Examiners' notes

Any essay on Realism, whether Left or Right should include a detailed discussion of their solutions to crime.

Examiners' notes

Left Realist solutions to crime should be cited in any essay which asks why the poor or ethnic minorities seem to commit more crime than other sections of society.

of elderly relatives in care homes because they suspect that carers may be stealing from or mistreating them.

- Fourthly, Foucault can be criticized because he under-estimates people's potential to resist the powerful's use of surveillance. For example, speed cameras are routinely vandalized, whilst criminals may simply move to areas in which there are fewer cameras. In this sense, surveillance may simply displace crime.

- Finally, Bigo and Guild conclude that surveillance has now moved into a new phase, which fits Beck's notion of a risk society. They note that surveillance has now taken on an exclusionary power in that it is now mainly used to sort and filter out those who put the rest of society at risk through the use of profiling. This type of surveillance is now becoming the norm in the social control of global movement. For example, the USA often refuses entry on the basis of profiling. It not only demands that visitors obtain a visa but that they also have a biometric passport. In 2016, Donald Trump announced his intention to ban all Muslims from entering the USA.

Environmental crime prevention

Environmental crime prevention (ECP) is very influenced by the Right Realist James Q Wilson who observed that crime is encouraged by the initial presence of 'incivilities' such as vandalism, graffiti, littering, dog fouling, swearing in public and so on. If these incivilities are not challenged or removed, this sends out a clear message to criminals that 'anything goes' and that the community is weak therefore encouraging more criminality. Wilson uses the example of broken windows. if these are not repaired immediately, vandals are encouraged to break more and perhaps motivated to indulge in other forms of anti-social behaviour.

Wilson notes that such incivilities are likely to occur if there is little sense of community or neighbourhood, as this means that both formal and informal social controls are usually weak. Members of the community may feel powerless and older members may be afraid to leave their homes. Respectable people may move away and more anti-social elements may replace them. The police may feel that anti-social behaviour is not their responsibility, as they target more serious types of crime. For further information on ECP and solutions such as zero tolerance policing, see pp 22–23.

Wilson says public housing estates are more likely to experience **social problems** such as drugs, graffiti and vandalism, and these are more likely to be found around high-rise tower blocks. He argues that these problems arise because residents do not take responsibility for the common entrances, stairwells and lifts. As a result, anti-social elements take over.

Social and community crime prevention

Left Realists argue that economic and social reform programmes need to be administered by governments if crime is to be seriously reduced in inner-city areas and on sink council estates. Left Realist ideas to reduce crime can be found on pp 24–25.

These policies should include:

- educational programmes aimed at improving educational success in inner-city comprehensives and reducing both exclusion and the number of 16-year-olds leaving school with no qualifications
- minimum pay legislation to ensure that people are paid a fair wage so that they are not tempted to become welfare-dependent
- reduction in wealth and income inequalities, e.g. through taxation
- economic investment in poorer urban communities to create jobs.

Generally, Left Realists argue that there should be a more coordinated attempt to improve people's economic and social opportunities. If people truly feel that the UK is meritocratic, they may be less likely to experience relative deprivation and powerlessness, and therefore the humiliation of poverty and the resulting resentment that fuels most crime.

However, these ideas have been criticized as being soft on crime and criminals, because they imply that crime is society's fault, rather than the individual's choice. Furthermore, Left Realists fail to explain why most people living in poverty do not commit crime. Right Realists argue that Left Realists make excuses for criminals, and that tighter controls, more effective socialization of children and more severe punishment are the main means by which society should reduce crime.

Punishment – pros and cons of prison

Most people believe that punishment, especially prison, is effective in preventing and reducing crime. They believe it can reduce crime in various ways:

	Way in which it reduces crime
Deterrence	The Right Realist position suggests that 'prison works', as prison deters many potential offenders away from crime; that is, it increases the costs of crime
Incapacitation	Right Realists argue that prison is important because it removes known criminals from the street so they cannot offend again. (Note: in some other societies, incapacitation can involve cutting off people's hands, chemical castration and capital punishment; in California, it has involved the 'three strikes and you're out' policy – committing even a minor third offence can lead to a lengthy prison sentence)
Rehabilitation	Some people believe that punishment can be used to reform or change offenders so that they will not return to their criminal careers; education and training in vocational skills are encouraged so that prisoners can earn an honest living once released

Table 5
Ways in which it is believed that prison can reduce crime

Does prison work?

The UK has invested heavily in prisons and, as a result, the prison population rose from about 60,000 in 1997 to 77,000 in 2006 and 83,000 in 2007. It was projected to rise to 90,000 by 2010 on current rates. The UK has more life-sentenced prisoners than the whole of the rest of Western Europe combined. Yet there is fierce debate about whether or not this policy is working.

Roger Matthews (1997) argues that the scale of imprisonment has little effect on the crime rate. He argues that, rather than reducing crime, prisons act as 'universities of crime' and that are an 'expensive way of making bad people worse'. At best, prisons are simply 'warehouses' in which the reasons for offending are very rarely addressed and little attempt is made to reform or rehabilitate the offender. He also points out that a substantial section of the prison population should not be in prison because they are either drug addicts or mentally ill, and need treatment rather than punishment.

E. Solomon (2006) suggests that many people are being imprisoned for relatively minor offences for which community punishments may be more suitable. Many people whose offences would not have attracted a custodial sentence in the past are now being sent to prison. Matthews suggests that up to 50% of the prison population have committed minor offences for which prison is inappropriate and possibly damaging.

Finally, the high rates of **recidivism** (repeat offending) suggest prison does not deter. Two-thirds of released prisoners reoffend, as do 71% of juvenile offenders, within two years of release. The overall evidence suggests prison is not radically changing the behaviour of repeat offenders.

Sociological perspectives on punishment

1. **Functionalism** – Durkheim claimed that punishment functioned to reaffirm the boundaries between conformist and deviant behaviour. For example, those who strayed into deviant behaviour would be punished in order to remind others of their duty to society. In this sense punishment served to maintain social unity and the collective conscience. Durkheim observed that, in societies characterized by mechanical solidarity (see p 4), punishment often took on a retributive character, Retribution means 'pay back' and is based on the idea that there should be a proportionate punishment for the offence committed; for example, 'an eye for an eye'. It is often found in traditional societies in which punishments are deliberately severe because the offender is seen to have transgressed against society rather than just another individual. The offender has broken the social rules which bond individuals together as a society. Retributive justice is deliberately severe because it has to convey the message that society is more important than the individual. In contrast, Durkheim saw 'restitutive justice' as mainly practised in societies characterized by organic solidarity. People in these societies are more individualistic but, despite this, are actually very dependent on one another. For example, we are dependent upon our neighbours not stealing our property. Restitutive justice views crime as an offence by

one individual against the rights of another. The victim has suffered a loss. Justice consists of the guilty offender making good the loss he or she has caused, to restore things to how they were before the offence occurred. The offender's debt, therefore, is not to society (as it is in societies that practise retributive justice) but, to the victim.

2. **Marxism** – Rushe and Kirchheimer argue that all punishment is an integral part of class struggle, between the bourgeoisie and proletariat, or today between global capital and the working poor. They believe that punishment does not benefit all of society (as functionalists argue). Rather, it assists the bourgeoisie or capitalist class in their efforts to materially dominate the working class. Marxists argue that punishments are mainly concerned with protecting the major priorities of capitalism. In the 18th century the major asset of capitalists was land, so 'crimes' against landed property such as poaching were often punished severely. In the 20th century money has become the main asset of capitalism; consequently crimes such as robbery are punished more severely than crimes against people, such as rape.

Essential notes

Think about the justice practised in Saudi Arabia, which is based on Sharia law and which still carries out public executions and amputations, as well as stoning women to death for adultery. Which type of justice is dominant?

Watts, Bessant and Hil (2008) argue that 'For most of the twentieth century criminologists paid much more attention to those defined as criminals and offenders than they did to the victims of criminal activity'. However, they suggest that this neglect ended in the 1970s and since then 'victimology' has become a major branch of the sociology of crime. This developing field has particularly focused upon the chances of being a victim of crime according to age, social class, gender, ethnicity and region.

The most influential contemporary approach to victimology is positivist victimology, which is mainly concerned with identifying patterns and trends in the distribution of victims across social groups such as social classes, age groups, men and women and ethnic minority groups. A good example of positivist victim studies are the victim surveys carried out annually by the Office for National Statistics (ONS) and the Home Office, known as the Crime Survey for England and Wales (CSEW). This survey has regularly concluded:

- The average person's chance of being a victim of crime is fairly low.
- Women worry more than men about being victims of crime, but young males are two times more likely to be victims of crime compared with females.
- The older a person gets, the less likely they are to be a victim of crime.
- People from ethnic minority backgrounds are more likely to be victims of crime compared with white people.
- Poorer households are more likely to be burgled that higher-income households.

However critical criminologists, who often come from Marxist or feminist backgrounds, are critical of positivist victim studies for a variety of reasons. In particular, they point out that positivists ignore structural factors such poverty, deprivation, power inequalities and patriarchy, which mean that groups such as the poor, ethnic minorities and women are at greater risk of victimization. The Left Realists Lea and Young surveyed victims of crime in inner-city areas and discovered that both the poor and women stood an above average chance of being repeat or regular victims of crime and that women's fear of sexual assault was well justified. Lea and Young criticize the sample – householders – used by the CSEW because it misses groups such as the homeless, who are 12 times more at risk of being victims of crime than those who own their own home, according to a survey carried out by Tim Newburn and Paul Rock.

Critical victimology

Marxist critics of positivist victimology argue that the general public are often unaware that they may have been victims of crimes committed by the powerful, such as corporate crime, green or environmental crime and state crime. Watts, Bessant and Hil argue that the victims identified in crime surveys are the victims 'that the state chooses to see'. They claim the state ignores those not readily identified as 'victims'. For example, victims of corporate, white-collar, state or green crimes are unlikely to appear in positivist victim surveys because questions which cover these types of offences are not included. The effects of such crimes on their victims is often complex and hidden so it is unlikely that victims would be aware of their victimhood anyway.

Critical victimologists also point out that whether a person is regarded as a 'victim' depends on their position in the power structures that underpin society. In this sense, victimhood is socially constructed, some victims of crime may be put off reporting crimes against them by the way the media, such as the popular newspapers, or the police treat victims. Sue Lees, for example, argues that both male and female victims of sexual offences such as rape never report the offences against them and so identify themselves as victims because they perceive that the societal reaction is likely to blame and stigmatize them for not doing enough to discourage the offender. Consequently they are never officially recognized as victims. The police play a key role in the social construction of victims. For example, some police officers may not treat domestic violence cases seriously. They may prefer to give the offender an unofficial warning and so deny the wife victim status.

Walklate argues that victimologists need to pay more attention to the role of the state. The state is important because it has the power to define who is regarded as a victim. Walklate says the state has the ultimate power to socially construct victimhood. A good example of this is the killing in July 2005 of a Brazilian man, Jean Charles de Menezes, was shot seven times in the head and killed by armed police officers who had mistaken him for a fugitive terrorist suspect. Despite the obvious injustice of his killing, de Menezes was not officially defined as a victim because the Crown Prosecution Service decreed there was too little evidence to prosecute the officers involved and because the coroner who chaired the inquest into his death refused to allow a verdict of unlawful killing. Such a response to a fatal shooting on the underground would be very unlikely if committed by anyone other than a representative of the state.

Critical criminologists who are feminists suggest that state definitions of what constitutes abuse against women may be limited in scope. For example, Kelly's research into 'survivors' of domestic violence found that many women were also undermined by verbal emotional abuse and bullying as well as physical violence. Sclater (2001) notes that some behaviour such as kicking and punching is easily recognizable as violent but behaviour currently not covered by the state's definitions, such as threats, verbal abuse, psychological manipulation or bullying and sexual intimidation, should also be categorized as domestic violence. Consequently many women who are victims of emotional and psychological abuse and bullying as well as sexual intimidation are not officially regarded as victims of domestic violence or abuse.

Evaluation of victimology

- New Right criminologists argue that critical victimology neglects their view that some victims may be responsible for crimes being committed against them, because they have not sufficiently invested in the technology required to make themselves 'harder targets' for criminals. However, this criticism does imply some unpleasant sexist ideas; for example, that some women are 'asking for it' because of the way they are dressed or because they are drunk.
- On a positive note, critical victimology has highlighted the role of power in how the status of victim is constructed.

Functionalism is very much associated with American sociology from roughly the 1930s to the 1960s, but its origins lie in the work of French sociologist Émile Durkheim, at the end of the 19th century.

Durkheim argued that most social phenomena and behaviour can only be explained by looking at the way societies are socially organized – at their social structures. Functionalism is therefore a **structuralist theory**.

Structuralist theories are generally also positivist theories. This means that they see human behaviour as being shaped by social forces, or social facts, beyond the control of the individual. In other words, people behave the way they do because the social forces bearing down on them propel them (possibly against their will) in a particular direction.

Functionalism sees society as being a social system that is made up of interdependent social institutions such as family, education, the political system, the criminal justice system and religion. Functionalists often use a biological analogy to describe how society works, likening it to the human body, with all its organs working together to bring about good health – just as all the social institutions of society work together to bring about social order.

Functionalists argue that capitalist societies are generally characterized by social order. According to functionalism, social order is dependent on four social processes.

1. Successful socialization into value consensus

Members of society learn the basic norms and values of society during primary socialization that occurs in the family. For example, children learn the difference between right and wrong and appropriate gender roles from their parents.

Secondary agents of socialization such as education systems are vital in that they transmit shared cultural values to produce conformity and consensus. For example, Durkheim believed that the teaching of subjects such as history, language and religious education link the individual to society, past and present, by promoting in the individual a sense of pride in the historical and religious achievements of their society or nation. Talcott Parsons argued that the main function of education was to act as a social bridge between the family unit and wider society. Education also socializes children into key values such as achievement, competition and individualism – functionalists see the transmission of these values as essential in preparing young people for the world of work.

Durkheim argued that the major function of religion is to socialize society's members into value consensus by investing certain values with a sacred quality, by infusing them with religious symbolism and special significance. These values become **moral codes** – beliefs that society agrees to revere and socialize children into. Such codes regulate our social behaviour with regard to crime, sexual behaviour and obligation to others.

2. Social integration

This refers to people's sense of belonging to society or a community. Socialization agencies such as education function to bring about a sense of social integration through the teaching of, for example, history and religion. The mass media may create the conditions for social integration by promoting nationalist or patriotic sentiments or by creating moral panics. Religion creates moral communities, which people identify with; for example, some people may see themselves primarily as Christian, Muslim or Jewish.

3. Social control

Once members of society have been socialized into values, their behaviour needs to be regulated and their values reinforced by informal agencies of control such as the family – for example, through praise and punishment – and religion, for example, through promises of heaven and threats of hell. Formal agencies of control such as the criminal justice system – for example, the police, the law, the judiciary and fear of imprisonment – also encourage people to conform to the rule of law.

4. Members of society are encouraged to take their place in the specialized division of labour as workers

Education encourages learning skills and attitudes through exams and qualifications, so that we can work in jobs that best suit our abilities; families encourage us to commit to a career.

However, Durkheim argued that value consensus is weaker in modern industrial societies because the complexity of modern life, especially urban life, has undermined the authority of religion and the family. Durkheim suggested that people in the modern world were more likely to experience anomie (moral confusion), meaning that they are less committed to society's rules and laws and therefore more likely to engage in actions that challenge value consensus that may be deviant or criminal.

Evaluation of functionalism

- It is **over-deterministic**, suggesting that behaviour is wholly determined by social factors. It does not consider free will, choice or the fact that action may depend upon how people interpret the social context in which they find themselves.
- It presents an over-socialized picture of people being turned into conformist citizens. However, some people may resist this process.
- It fails to account for the social conflict that exists in modern societies – for example, critics argue that it places too much emphasis on consensus and order, although Durkheim's concept of anomie did anticipate the potential for social conflict.
- It fails to consider the possible social dysfunctions of key social institutions, such as the domestic violence that occurs in some families.

Essential notes

Specialized division of labour refers to the range of skills or jobs that exist in a particular society. All workers play a crucial role in ensuring that society works efficiently. Imagine life without, for example, trained doctors, sewage workers, electricians, supermarket workers or cleaners.

Examiners' notes

In 20-mark essay questions you may be asked to assess the contribution of functionalism to our understanding of the way society is organized. Remember to summarize and evaluate functionalism if the Theory and Method exam question focuses on structuralist or macro theories. When evaluating, try to contrast functionalism with Marxism or social action theory or postmodernism.

Marxism

Marxism is a structuralist theory too, in that it argues that the organization or structure of capitalist society, especially the fact that such societies are based on social class relationships, is the main influence on the behaviour of social groups such as the working class.

Marxism sees capitalist society as organized into two interdependent parts. The infrastructure is the economic system – the way society produces goods. In capitalist societies, goods are manufactured mainly in factories. This production involves a relationship between two economic classes – the bourgeoisie or capitalist class own the means of production (land, factories and machines); the **proletariat** or working class hires out its labour power (its skills, stamina and strength) to the capitalist class in return for a wage.

The relationship between these two classes is unequal and is based on conflict, because the bourgeoisie aim to extract maximum labour at the lowest cost. As a result, the bourgeoisie exploit the labour of the working class, especially because the value of labour when sold as a product is worth more than the wage paid. This gap between the value of labour-power and wages is known as **surplus value**. It is pocketed by the capitalist class and is the basis of vast profits made by many employers. These profits are responsible for the great inequalities in wealth and income between the ruling and working classes.

The second part of the capitalist social system – the superstructure – is made up of social institutions such as the family, education and mass media. Marxists argue that capitalist societies are inherently unstable because of the potential for conflict between the social classes. The function of the superstructure is to transmit ruling class ideology aimed at convincing the working-class that society is **meritocratic** and fair. Such ideology also functions to justify inequality as well as to hide away the conflicts of interest that divide the working class from the capitalist class. Consequently the working class accept their unequal position in society as natural and inevitable. Ruling-class ideology eventually results in **false class-consciousness** – workers are unaware that they are being exploited and that society is unfairly loaded against them. This ensures working-class conformity and class inequalities in areas such as income, education and health that are reproduced generation after generation.

Marxists are therefore suggesting that working-class behaviour is constrained and shaped by the class inequality that characterizes the infrastructure and the ideology produced by the superstructure. However, Karl Marx believed that workers would eventually become politically conscious of capitalist inequality and exploitation and collectively take revolutionary action against the capitalist class.

Evaluation of Marxism

- Critics argue that Marxists put too much emphasis on conflict. Even if the infrastructure is exploitative, capitalism has improved the standard of living of the working class, who may be aware of inequality and exploitation but feel that their improved standard of living compensates for this. They may therefore actively choose to carry on cooperating with capitalism because it has benefited them in terms of economic standards, education, welfare and health care.

- Weber and others have criticized Marx for economic reductionism – this means he reduces all social behaviour to class relationships. However, social behaviour can also be influenced by religious, patriarchal, nationalistic and ethnic structures and relationships.
- Marx's description of capitalism and its inevitable move towards revolution has simply not occurred. Indeed, capitalism has grown stronger and, through globalization, has spread across the world.
- Marx predicted a **polarization** of people in capitalist society into a tiny rich minority and an extremely poor majority, but this has not occurred. There are great wealth and income inequalities, but there has also been massive middle-class growth, which Marx did not anticipate.

Neo-Marxism

Louis Althusser focused on the role of the state and argued that it was composed of two elements: repressive state apparatuses composed of the coercive institutions such as the police and the army; and ideological state apparatuses such as the education system, the mass media and religion, which socialize the working class into passive acceptance of their lot and, consequently, false class-consciousness. Herbert Marcuse argues that our wants, needs and desires are manipulated by the media, and especially advertising, in order to increase profits by selling even more capitalist commodities. Marcuse argues that the function of the media is to ensure that the minds of the masses are focused on trivial entertainment rather than on any critical analysis of capitalism.

Some neo-Marxists are critical of the economic determinism of traditional Marxism. They argue that social behaviour is not always shaped by the economic system. Antonio Gramsci believed that ideas could exist independently of both the infrastructure and the superstructure, which could challenge the hegemony or cultural dominance of the bourgeoisie. These ideas have been developed by the 'New Criminology' (see pp 14–15), which sees criminal behaviour as a form of political resistance to capitalist inequality.

However, David Harvey notes that in the past 20 years capitalism has gone through major organizational changes. He notes that globalization has helped to create whole new areas of commerce and thus new sources of profit. In particular, transnational corporations are exploiting the labour power of developing nations to produce cheap goods for marketing in the affluent West. He suggests that states are now less powerful than global institutions such as transnationals and the World Trade Organization. Finally, Harvey argues that social class as the dominant source of inequality is likely to be replaced in the future by divisions linked to gender, ethnicity, religion, and even alternative political movements such as the green movement.

Essential notes

Marxism is a type of conflict theory because the two main social groupings – the bourgeoisie and the proletariat – are in fundamental conflict with each other, which Marx claimed could only be resolved by the proletariat becoming fully class-conscious and adopting revolutionary means to overthrow the bourgeoisie.

Examiners' notes

In Theory and Method questions, you may be asked to assess the contribution of Marxism to our understanding of the way society is organized. Remember to summarize and evaluate Marxism if the Theory and Method exam question focuses on structuralist, conflict or macro theories. When evaluating Marxism, try to contrast it with functionalism or social action theory or postmodernism.

Essential notes

Neo-Marxists are influenced by interpretivism, so they are interested in how people interpret their experience of social class, exploitation and inequality. This is therefore a theory that can be used in support of social action or interpretivist perspectives if you are asked such a Theory and Method question.

Essential notes

Feminist theories are generally focused on how society is organized along patriarchal lines. Moreover, they are interested in showing how social institutions such as the family and the media are shaping women's lives. So, in this sense, feminist theories tend to be structuralist, positivist and macro in character. Furthermore, feminism, like Marxism, is a conflict theory, because it sees conflict between men and women.

Examiners' notes

The ability to distinguish between the different theoretical strands of feminism can lift an essay response into the top mark band.

Examiners' notes

Note that Marxist feminism would also be relevant to any Theory and Method exam question on Marxism.

Feminism focuses on the conflict between men and women and the social structure of patriarchy (male domination, female subordination and therefore gender inequality) that characterizes the organization of modern societies. It focuses on gender inequalities in education and employment, social mobility, political power and family relationships. Broadly speaking, there are three types of feminism.

1. Liberal feminism

Liberal feminists see society as patriarchal but suggest that women's opportunities are improving because of the **feminization of the economy** (the **service sector**, particularly financial services and retail, has become dominated by a female workforce), improved educational achievement and a radical change in social attitudes that Helen Wilkinson calls a **genderquake**. She notes that the aspirations of the present female generation are radically different from those of their mothers and grandmothers. The current generation are not content to accept that their lives should be solely defined and shaped by domestic and family roles. Evidence from surveys conducted by Sue Sharpe suggest that young women are more demanding today with regard to their educational and career ambitions. They are now more likely than previous generations to see themselves as equals to men.

Liberal feminists also note that marriage has become more egalitarian because women now have reproductive rights (with access to contraception and abortion, which allows them to control their fertility), divorce, and economic power derived from large-scale entry into employment and better wages. Furthermore, they argue that gender-role socialization in families is slowly changing in favour of females, as parents no longer view their daughters as second-class citizens or encourage them to see themselves as subordinate to their brothers. Liberal feminists are therefore optimistic about the future of females in modern societies.

2. Marxist feminism

Marxist feminists such as Margaret Benston see patriarchy as an ideological aspect of capitalism. They argue that the bourgeoisie use gender to divide and rule the male and female working class. Patriarchal ideology transmits the idea that women are inferior or subordinate to men and this makes it easier for capitalism to control and exploit men and women.

Benston argues that capitalism transmits the idea that women's family role as mothers and housewives is their most important function because women's **domestic labour** is crucial to capitalism in two important respects. First, capitalism requires a future workforce – it is the role of the mother-housewife to reproduce and to bring up the future workforce free of charge for the capitalist class. Second, the present workforce requires maintenance – it needs to be fed and its batteries recharged to be efficient. The housewife role maintains the health and efficiency of the male workforce at no extra cost to the capitalist class.

Other Marxist feminists see women as part of a **reserve army of labour**, which is only hired by capitalist enterprises in times of rapid economic expansion, but fired when recession sets in. Marxists argue that women are vulnerable to trends such as economic recession, downsizing and mergers, and so make up a more disposable part of the workforce.

3. Radical feminism

Radical feminists such as Christine Delphy argue that gender inequality is more important than class inequality. They argue that society is divided into two basic gender classes – men and women – whose interests are opposed. Modern societies are patriarchal societies, in which men exploit and oppress women in all aspects of social life. Culture, government, tradition, religion, law, education and the media all reflect patriarchal ideology and power.

All these types of patriarchal inequality originate, not in wider society, but in the intimacy of personal relationships, and especially in the gender-role socialization found in families. Radical feminists note that patriarchal ideology is used to control women for the benefit of men. Women are told how to look, dress and behave. When patriarchal ideology fails, then women are always under the threat of male violence and sexual aggression, which limits their capacity to live as free and independent beings.

Evaluation of feminism

- Like functionalism and Marxism, feminism is **over deterministic** – it suggests that social behaviour is wholly determined by social factors beyond the control of females. It does not take choice or how females interpret their social situation into consideration. Catherine Hakim notes that some women may be happy to be mothers and housewives.
- It presents an over-socialized picture of women being turned into conformist mothers or housewives. In this sense, Marxist and radical feminism are outdated and fail to consider recent changes such as genderquake, educational success or new jobs have benefited women.
- Marxist feminists believe that domestic labour benefits capitalism, but Sylvia Walby (1986) is critical of this approach. She argues that women staying at home harms capitalism, because if women competed with men for jobs this might lower wages and increase profits. Women who earn also have superior spending power, which boosts capitalism.
- The reserve army of labour theory fails to explain why there are men's jobs and women's jobs and why women end up with responsibility for domestic labour.
- Feminism neglects the influence of social class and ethnicity. Middle-class women may not be exploited by men as much as working-class women, because they have more access to education and economic power, which means they might be able to resist patriarchal influences. The influence of factors such as religion or racism could mean that black or Asian women experience more exploitation than white women. These criticisms have led to what has become known as **difference feminism**.

Examiners' notes

Use examples from other areas of the specification to illustrate these ideas. For example, you could look at the lack of women in top jobs or in politics, or at the way women are represented in the mass media or in world religions.

Examiners' notes

In the 20-mark Theory and Methods question on Paper 3 of the A-level, you may be asked to assess the contribution of feminism to our understanding of the way society is organized. Note that you will need to summarize and evaluate the three types of feminism if the Theory and Method question focuses on patriarchal, conflict or macro theories. When evaluating feminism, use the specific criticisms but also contrast feminism with functionalism, Marxism, social action theory and postmodernism.

Essential notes

Be aware that social action theories may sometimes be called 'interpretivist', 'interactionist' or 'phenomenological' theories.

Social action theorists (also known as **interpretivists**) reject the assumption held by structuralist sociology – functionalist and Marxist sociologists – that social behaviour is constrained and even made predictable by the organization of society. Social action theorists see people as having a much more proactive role in shaping social life.

Social action theorists reject the view that people's behaviour is the product of external forces over which they have little control. Chris Brown argues that people actually engage in voluntary behaviour. Most people do not feel themselves to be the puppets of society.

However, although people operate as individuals, they are aware of other people around them. Social action theorists argue that the attitudes and actions of others influence the way people think and behave. Social action theorists also argue that society is the product of people choosing to come together and interacting in social groups and trying to make sense of their own and each other's behaviour. In this sense people's choices and the social meanings they apply to interaction mean that they socially construct society. They are the architect rather than the puppets of society.

Essential notes

Social action theories are **micro theories**, in that they are more concerned with how individuals interpret the social world around them than with examining the way society is structured or organized. They are therefore **anti-positivist**.

People are able to work out what is happening in any given situation because they bring a set of interpretations to every **social interaction** and use them to make sense of social behaviour or social meanings. In particular, people apply meanings to symbolic behaviour. When they interact with others, they are on the lookout for symbols, because these give clues as to how the other person is interpreting their behaviour. For example, smiling is symbolic behaviour that might be interpreted as social approval.

Experience of **symbolic interaction** results in people acquiring knowledge about what is appropriate behaviour in particular situations. They learn that particular contexts demand particular social responses. For example, drinking and dancing at a party is regarded as appropriate, yet the same behaviour at a funeral is probably inappropriate.

Socialization and identity

Social action theorists argue that socialization involves learning a stock of shared interpretations and meanings for most given social interactions. Families, for example, teach children how to interact with and interpret the actions of others.

Essential notes

Social action approaches do not necessarily deny the existence of roles, norms and values. However, they tend to see them as flexible rules rather than rigid frameworks over which we have no control. Thus our roles, such as brothers, sisters, mothers, fathers, children, students or workers, are open to individual interpretation and negotiation.

Social action theorists suggest that socialization results in individuals acquiring a social identity, which refers to the personality characteristics and qualities that particular cultures associate with certain social roles or groups. In British culture, for example, mothers are expected to be loving, nurturing and selfless, so women who are mothers will attempt to live up to this description and acquire this social identity. As children grow up, socialization and interaction with others will show them what British culture expects of them in terms of obligations, duties and behaviour towards others.

Furthermore, the individual has a subjective sense of her or his uniqueness and identity. Sociologists call this the **self**. It is partly the product of what others think is expected of a person's social identity. However, 'self' is also the product of how the individual interprets her or his experience and life history. For example, some women may have, in their own minds, serious misgivings about their role as mother. The self, then, is the link between what society expects from a particular role and the individual's interpretation of whether she or he is living up to that role successfully.

The concept of self has been explored extensively by social action sociologists. Some have suggested that the self has two parts – the 'I' and the 'me'. The 'I' is the private inner self, whereas the 'me' is the social self that participates in everyday interaction. When a person plays a social role as a teacher or student, the 'me' is in action. The 'me' is shaped by the reactions of others – that is, people act in ways they think are socially desirable. However, the 'I' supplies the confidence or self-esteem to play the role successfully.

Key study

Erving Goffman – everyday life as role-playing

Erving Goffman (1959) argues that social interaction is about successful **role-playing**.

He suggests that we are all social actors engaged in the drama of everyday life. Stage directions are symbolized by the social and cultural context in which the action takes place. For example, the classroom as a stage symbolizes particular rules that must be followed if the interaction is to be successful. For example, students sit at desks while teachers can move around the room freely.

Labelling theory is a type of social action theory, which points out that although there is a consensus of meaning on how people should behave, it is constantly evolving and changing. For example, interactionists argue there is no such thing as 'right' or 'wrong' behaviour. However, some groups have more power and are able to impose their meanings or interpretations on the rest of us. They make the rules (for example, laws), which define the behaviour of other groups as deviant or criminal. They are able to apply negative labels via the mass media (via moral panics), education (for example, the ideal student stereotype) and through the legal system (for example, police officers on the beat may use stereotypes of what they think is the typical criminal or suspicious person when deciding who to stop and search). Interactionists point out that labels, applied by means of education or policing, have a powerful effect on the self-esteem and status of groups such as ethnic minorities and can bring about self-fulfilling prophecies and deviant subcultural responses.

Evaluation social action theory

- The main weakness of social action theory lies in its failure to explore the wider social factors that create the context in which symbols, self and interaction all exist, for example, class, race and patriarchy. This means that it has no explanation for where the symbolic meanings or labels/stereotypes originate.
- It also completely fails to explore power differences between groups and individuals, and why these might occur. For example, Marxists argue that capitalism gives the ruling class the power to impose its interpretations of reality on less powerful groups in society, such as the working class or poor.

Examiners' notes

In the Theory and Method essay questions, you may be asked to assess the contribution of social action theory to our understanding of the way society is organized. You should summarize and evaluate social action theory if the question focuses on interactionist, interpretivist or micro theories. When evaluating social action theory, try to contrast it with structuralist theories in general or functionalism, Marxism or feminism.

Postmodernists argue that the history of British society can be divided into two broad periods. The 20th century was dominated by the modern industrial period – modern society. However, towards the latter end of the 20th century – the 1980s – society began to evolve into the postmodern period. The two periods differ from each other in important ways.

The modern or industrial period was characterized by seven key features:

1. Industrialization was organized along capitalist lines. Mainly, people were employed in heavy industries such as coal, iron and steel and shipbuilding, or in factories, manufacturing products such as cars, textiles and electrical items.
2. Social class was the major source of most people's identity in that the capitalist ruling class owned the factories, the middle classes managed them and the working class worked in them. Generally, people were proud to identify themselves using class labels, and differences in values and lifestyles were clearly class differences.
3. Traditional social institutions such as the family, the workplace and religion wield great influence over people's sense of identity. The individual is seen as less important than the larger group – family, religion, nation state – to which he or she belongs.
4. **Urbanization** resulted, as industrialization saw mass migration from rural areas to the urban centres in search of factory work. People lived in impersonal urban areas in which the sense of community was weak.
5. The state or government extended its influence over a range of aspects of people's lives. In modern society, the government takes responsibility for the education, health and welfare of people from the cradle to the grave.
6. Scientific or rational thinking became more important than irrational belief systems such as religion. The modernist theory of positivism, which argues that the scientific approach is the only approach to take in solving society's problems and improving living standards, becomes dominant.
7. Big ideas or **metanarratives** developed – for example, political theories such as socialism, as well as sociological theories such as functionalism, Marxism and feminism – in order to explain how modern society works. For example, in the 19th century, positivist sociology developed as a theory that aimed to explain the modern industrial world using the principles of scientific logic.

However, postmodernists believe that the modern world is dissolving and has been replaced with postmodern ideas and institutions.

Distinguishing the postmodern world from the modern world

This postmodern world has various characteristics that distinguish it from the modern world.

- The nature of work has dramatically changed – the primary sector (such as coal mining) and secondary sectors (such as factory work) of the economy have declined because of globalization – raw materials can be extracted and goods can be manufactured more cheaply in China and the developing world. The tertiary or service economy (such as the financial, state and retail sectors) has become the dominant segment of the British economy. As a result of these changes in the economy, social class, which traditionally was the major source of identity in Britain, has allegedly gone into decline.

- Postmodern societies are 'media-saturated' societies – magazines, television, cinema, pop music and social networking sites on the internet such as Facebook, Twitter and Instagram have all become central to the way we live our lives.
- Globalization is also a norm in postmodern societies. This means that we are now more exposed to, for example, global brands, icons, music, films, food and drink than ever before. This combination of media saturation, popular culture and globalisation means that people have more choices available to them in terms of constructing their identity.
- The consumption of consumer goods, especially the conspicuous consumption of designer goods, is increasingly an important aspect of personal identity.
- The modernist metanarratives or grand explanations that explain why society or the world works in the way that it does, such as science, socialism and feminism, have lost their power and influence. For example, people have become sceptical, even cynical, about the power of science to change the world, as many of the world's problems are seen to have been caused by science and technology.
- Postmodernists now argue that there is no such thing as 'truth' – all knowledge is relative and has something to contribute to our understanding of how society works. Sociology, therefore, is only one set of ideas that must compete with others.

Evaluation of postmodernism

- Critics of postmodernism argue that it probably exaggerates the degree of economic and social change; for example, the majority of workers in the UK still work in the manufacturing industry.
- Ulrich Beck claims that Western societies have entered a second age of modernity rather than the postmodern age. This second age is characterized by globalization and individualization (greater pursuit of self-interest). These societies are also characterized by 'risk'. Science and technology have brought society great benefits in terms of improving standards of living, but they have brought about 'manufactured risks' in the form of environmental pollution, global warming, increased risk of disasters and diseases such as cancer.
- Evidence suggests that social class remains important as a source of identity – surveys indicate that people still see social class as a strong subjective influence in their lives.
- Postmodernists ignore the fact that the nature of people's consumption – what and how much they consume – still very much depends on their income, which depends on the job they have and their social class.
- People's ability to make choices is also still influenced by traditional constraints stressed by modernists, such as gender, age and ethnicity. For example, women are still paid on average 80% of men's earnings and still have to negotiate a glass ceiling in their attempt to get access to top jobs, while ethnic minorities still face the daily experience of racism in all its shapes and forms.

Essential notes

It is important to clearly link positivist methodology to positivist beliefs about the causes of social behaviour; it is also essential to highlight crucial positivist concepts such as standardization, **reliability**, objectivity and quantifiability.

Positivists are very influenced by the natural sciences. Natural scientists such as biologists, physicists and chemists have shown us that plants, animals and chemicals behave in predictable ways because of natural laws. For example, water obeys predictable physical laws when heated up and chemicals react in predictable ways when they are mixed with other chemicals. Positivist sociologists have adapted and applied these ideas to human behaviour, arguing that we should treat people as objects whose behaviour can be observed and counted in the same way as animals, the weather and chemical elements.

Positivists see human behaviour as the product of the organization of the society in which we live. They argue that the structure of society produces social laws (sometimes called '**social facts**') over which we have no control or choice and which determine our behaviour; they see people as the puppets of society. Positivists argue that social behaviour is patterned, in that groups of people behave in similar, and therefore predictable, ways.

Positivists believe that sociology should adopt the logic and research methods of the natural sciences to research human behaviour. This means that they believe that:

- Sociologists should study only what they can objectively see, measure and count.
- Research subjects should be exposed to standardized stimuli under controlled conditions.
- Reliability should be high – according to Crossman (2016), reliability is the degree to which a measuring instrument or research method gives the same results each time that it is used. A method is very reliable if, for example, another sociologist is able to use the same or a very similar method to repeat a particular piece of research in order to verify its results.
- Research methods should produce quantifiable or statistical data.
- Statistical relationships (that is, **correlations**) can be established between various factors, which, if confirmed, can be classified as 'social laws or facts' that explain the causes of patterned social behaviour.

Key study

Émile Durkheim and suicide

Émile Durkheim produced the classic sociological study *Le Suicide* in 1897, to illustrates two key ideas.

1. Durkheim was a positivist sociologist, who believed that even a supremely 'individual' act such as suicide was influenced by society.
2. He believed that sociology was a science. His study of suicide was intended as an illustration of scientific enquiry in sociology.

As his main source of data, Durkheim used 19th-century official statistics of suicide taken from a range of European societies for the period 1840–70. He noted three trends:

1. Within single societies the suicide rate remains constant over time.
2. The suicide rate varies constantly between different societies.

3. The suicide rate varies constantly between different groups within the same society.

Durkheim argued that constancy of suicide rates across Europe meant that they were social facts, determined or shaped by the nature or structure of societies.

Durkheim used the **comparative method**, comparing sets of official statistics to discover the social phenomena responsible for suicide rates.

Firstly, Durkheim looked at possible non-social influences on suicide such as climate, heredity, alcoholism and mental illness, but concluded that none of these profoundly affected the suicide rate.

After examining possible social **variables**, Durkheim produced the following **hypothesis**: 'the suicide rate varies inversely according to the degree of social integration and **moral regulation** of the social group of which the individual is a part.'

Durkheim identified three major types of suicide that he argued were the product of the way societies were organized. The most important type was **'egoistic' suicide**, which he argued resulted from individuals experiencing a lack of social integration. Durkheim believed that people who commit egoistic suicide do not experience a strong sense of community. They suffer from an 'excess of individualism'. Durkheim suggested that some people were better integrated into society because of religious and family influences.

For example, Durkheim noted that Catholic societies have lower suicide rates than Protestant societies. He concluded that this is because Catholics feel a stronger sense of community than Protestants. Durkheim claimed that Catholics have a stronger sense of their religious identity and their place within the Catholic community, whereas the Protestant encouragement of 'free will' means that Protestants are not as committed to the notion of religious community.

He also noted that suicide rates showed that married people with children are more protected from suicide than single or divorced people or childless couples. Durkheim suggested that the protection comes not from marriage itself, but from the integrating effects of family life and children.

Another thing Durkheim observed was that suicide rates tended to decline in times of war or political upheaval. This is because more individuals identify themselves with a 'common cause'. They become more patriotic and nationalistic, and therefore more integrated into collective life and, at least temporarily, less vulnerable to suicide.

Durkheim's second type of suicide **'altruistic' suicide** is the opposite of egoistic suicide. He argued that it is caused by the over-integration of the individual into the social group. In altruistic suicide, the individual's ego, rather than being too great, is too weak to resist the

Essential notes

Durkheim's theory of suicide is also a good example of functionalism in action. He believed that a key symptom of **anomie** in societies characterized by organic solidarity was a high or increasing suicide rate. He therefore hoped to show that suicide was somehow connected to the failure of social mechanisms to integrate and regulate the behaviour of individuals, thus confirming a key functionalist idea – that there is a functional relationship between weak-value consensus, social order and deviance. In contrast, in societies in which there is strong consensus and a strong sense of belonging, suicide rates ought to be low.

☞ **This topic continues on the next six pages**

Examiners' notes

If you are faced with a Theory and Method question on the functionalist theory of society or consensus theory, use Durkheim's theory of suicide as illustration. Be aware too that suicide is regarded as a type of deviance because it is not 'normal' behaviour; therefore an essay question which asks you to evaluate the functionalist theory of crime and deviance can legitimately discuss suicide (deviance) as well as crime.

demands of society, so that the individual feels he or she must commit suicide. Recent examples of such suicides include suicide bombers and the mass suicides committed by religious sects such as 'People's Temple'.

A third type of suicide identified was **'anomic' suicide**, which arises from the lack of regulation of the individual by society. For example, in times of rapid economic change, individuals might find themselves in radically changed circumstances. A wealthy person who has suddenly become poor because of, for example, a stock market crash may not be able to cope with the new set of norms and values he or she must deal with. The confusion or anomie experienced can result in suicidal action.

Durkheim's theory of suicide has been subject to criticism:

- It has been suggested that suicide statistics collected between 1840 and 1870 are not reliable, because there was no systematic medical examination of the dead in many parts of Europe until the late 19th century.
- Durkheim failed to explain why suicide is the most likely result of not enough or too much integration – why not some other course of action, such as crime?
- Durkheim did not offer any guidance on how to recognize different types of suicide. **Interpretivist sociologists** note that, without knowing the intention of the deceased, it is difficult to use Durkheim's classification.

Experiments

In many of the natural sciences, the laboratory **experiment** is the main means by which scientists gather data and test theories.

Scientists like experiments because they are conducted in a controlled environment. In a laboratory experiment, the researcher is interested in the relationship between an **independent variable** (a possible cause) and a **dependent variable** (a possible effect). The experiment involves setting up two identical groups – an experimental group and a **control group** – which are treated differently. The experimental group is exposed to the independent variable and its behaviour is often compared to the control group (which is not exposed) to monitor any differences between the two. Any differences are seen as dependent variables or effects.

Positivists regard the laboratory experiment as reliable for three reasons:

1. The original researcher can control the conditions and specify the precise steps that were used in the original experiment, so others can easily repeat the steps to rerun it.
2. It produces quantitative data, so the results of the rerun experiment can be compared to the original easily.
3. It is a detached and objective method – the researcher merely manipulates the variables and records the results.

Essential notes

Laboratory experiments tend not to be suitable for sociological research, but psychologists have used them extensively. For example, Albert Bandura used laboratory experiments to test the idea that violent media content could cause children to be violent in real life.

Evaluating laboratory experiments

There are practical, ethical and theoretical reasons why sociologists are not keen on using laboratory experiments.

- Humans are complex beings, so it is impossible to construct identical human experimental and control groups. No two humans are exactly alike, because we experience and interpret all social situations in different ways.
- Laboratory experiments can only focus on small samples and so are not that useful in studying large-scale social phenomena.
- A laboratory experiment is an artificial environment and any behaviour that occurs in it may be a product of the environment. The subjects may act differently: for example, they may feel self-important, anxious or resentful, or they may work out what the researcher wants and give it to them. This is the **Hawthorne effect**, named after experiments conducted by Mayo in the 1920s at the Hawthorne factory in the USA where it was first observed.
- Experiments may result in the harming of research subjects. For example, exposing children to violent films for long periods may result in long-term psychological or emotional damage.
- Interpretivists argue that humans are fundamentally different from other natural phenomena. We have free will and the ability to choose how to behave. Our behaviour is not 'caused' by external forces beyond our control, so it cannot be explained in terms of cause-and-effect relationships.

Positivists prefer research methods that produce data in numerical form. Their preferred primary method of research is the social survey, which most commonly uses questionnaires or structured interviews to collect data. They also like to use secondary data such as official statistics, collected by government sources.

Social surveys

A social survey involves collecting large amounts of statistical data from many people, usually via questionnaires or structured interviews.

Some surveys may be **longitudinal research**, which means that the same group of people may be surveyed over a long period of time. These provide a clear image of changes in attitudes and behaviour over time, but can be problematic, because respondents may die, drop out or researchers may lose track of them. The views of those that remain in the sample may also be significantly different from the views of those who drop out, so over time the sample may become increasingly unrepresentative.

Questionnaires

A questionnaire is simply a list of questions that are written down in advance. They are the main method for gathering data in social surveys. They are handed out or posted to the respondent – the person chosen by the researcher to answer the questions. They are also found in magazines and are now increasingly posted online. Most questionnaires are self-completion questionnaires. Others may be read out and filled in on behalf of the respondent by trained interviewers. This type of questionnaire or **interview schedule** is known as the formal or structured interview.

Examiners' notes

The laboratory experiment is regarded as the ultimate methodology by positivists, so you could use the arguments about the strengths and weaknesses of this method in Theory and Method exam questions that ask you to examine the positivist versus interpretivist debate.

Essential notes

Surveys generally aim to find out facts about a population or uncover differences in beliefs or social attitudes or test a hypothesis. For example, every 10 years the government conducts the **Census**, when a questionnaire is sent out to every household in the UK, to uncover facts about British lifestyles.

Examiners' notes

You should know some strengths and weaknesses of longitudinal surveys, as they tend to be asked in short exam questions.

Examiners' notes

It is important to clearly define what is meant by a questionnaire and to explain how one is usually organized.

Essential notes

It is important to conduct a **pilot survey**, to resolve possible questionnaire problems. This entails testing the questions on a small group of people who share the characteristics of the main sample. A pilot survey is useful to check that the questions are clear and do not upset or lead the participants, that the sampling technique used will target the 'right' types of people to fill in the questionnaire, that the researchers are well trained and that the data produced is the kind that is wanted.

Essential notes

Some survey questionnaires may also use questions based on the Likert scale. These aim to measure people's attitudes by offering a choice of pre-coded responses to a series of statements that aim to measure strength or weakness of subjective feelings about a social event or issue. For example, 'On a scale of 1–5, to what extent do you agree or disagree with the following statement?' Options might include strongly agree, agree, neither agree nor disagree, disagree, strongly disagree.

When constructing a questionnaire, the sociologist must ensure that the right questions are asked to unearth the exact information that is needed. So the questions must focus on the hypothesis. Turning the hypothesis into a series of questions is called 'operationalization'.

Ideally, questions should be objective and it is essential that they contain neutral wording. However, questions can be biased, in that they can 'lead' respondents to the answers the researcher requires. They can sometimes be 'loaded', or written in such a way that the respondent is provoked into an emotional response that seeks to evade the truth.

Questionnaires tend to use **'closed' questions** with a choice of pre-set answers with accompanying tick boxes, which produce quantitative data. Questionnaires have a number of strengths and weaknesses, as shown in the table below.

Questionnaires – strengths
• If postal, can be used to reach large numbers of people around the country, which may improve the representativeness of the sample (e.g. sociologists might want to compare how people in Scotland view crime compared to people in England or Wales) • They are less time-consuming for respondents than interviews • Reasonably cheap compared to other methods • Useful for research that includes sensitive or embarrassing questions, as these can be answered in the privacy of the home rather than face-to-face, which might undermine validity • Ensure that the sociologist has minimum contact with the respondent, so reducing the possibility of the respondent feeling suspicious or threatened

Questionnaires – weaknesses
• Especially if postal, suffer from low response or even **non-response** • Those returned may not be representative of the research population, as the replies may be from people with strong unrepresentative views • May not be suitable for finding out why people behave the way they do, as real life is often too complex to categorize in closed questions and responses • Respondents may interpret questions in a different way from that intended by the researcher • Artificial devices that are not a normal part of daily reality, so people may respond with suspicion and may not tell the truth, or may be partial, as they feel threatened by the research or researchers • By choosing the questions and responses, the researcher has already mapped out the experiences and interpretations of respondents (e.g. they may be forced to tick boxes that only approximate to their experiences, views and opinions, thus undermining the validity of the data, which may frustrate respondents and result in non-response)

Table 6
Strengths and weaknesses of questionnaires

Self-report questionnaires

In an attempt to uncover the true amount of crime in society, some criminologists have used a type of questionnaire called a self-report. It lists various petty criminal acts and asks respondents to tick those they have committed without being caught. Sociologists attempt to improve validity by stressing confidentiality and anonymity for the respondents.

Marsh notes that the validity of self-reporting is undermined by under-reporting and over-reporting. People may under-report because self-report studies are retrospective and depend on being able to remember crimes committed 12 months before. Some people, especially boys, may exaggerate offences to create a 'tough' impression. Others keep quiet, as they fear that the police will be informed.

The representativeness of self-report questionnaires is questioned for three reasons:

1. It is impossible to include all criminal acts in a questionnaire. This means the researcher must be selective, which raises problems as to which offences should or should not be included.
2. Self-reports are distributed mainly to young people – it would be difficult to get businesspeople to cooperate and admit in a self-report questinnaire to various types of white-collar or corporate crime.
3. Josine Junger-Tas (1989) reports a sliding scale of responses to self-report questionnaires, depending on how much contact respondents have had with the criminal justice system. **Response rates** from people with a criminal record were lower than from those without.

Structured interviews

Positivists also view formal or structured interviews as a scientific method. These interviews usually involve the researcher reading out a list of closed questions from an interview schedule – a type of questionnaire – and ticking boxes or writing down answers according to pre-set fixed categories on behalf of the respondent. The interviewer plays a passive role, acting as a recording machine, and may not deviate from the interview schedule questions.

The Crime Survey of England and Wales (CSEW) of 2015–16 conducted about 50,000 structured interviews with a sample of people aged 16 and over, living in private households in England and Wales. Using laptop computers, 22 trained interviewers recorded the responses.

In many ways, structured interviews are similar to questionnaires, so they share some of the same strengths, but although they share the same problems as questionnaires some of these are unique to this method. The advantages and disadvantages are as follows.

Essential notes

Positivists regard questionnaire surveys as scientific, as they are standardized, objective, reliable and collect mainly quantitative data, which can be compared easily for correlations. There are also few ethical problems with questionnaires, especially if delivered via the post, as returning them indicates that respondents have given their consent.

Essential notes

Pilot surveys are essential in order to avoid this problem.

Essential notes

The danger exists that questionnaires might be completed in a group rather than by the individual alone. Responses may reflect peer group pressure rather than own views.

Essential notes

There will always be some social groups who will never respond positively to a questionnaire because they are 'deviant' and associate questionnaires with authority.

Structured interviews – advantages	Structured interviews – disadvantages
The focus on closed questions and fixed categories means they are very useful for collecting straightforward factual data	Inflexible, as the questionnaire or interview schedule is drawn up in advance and the interviewer must stick to it rigidly; interpretivists note that this makes it impossible to pursue interesting leads that may emerge during the interview
Can use relatively large samples, as they can be conducted fairly quickly (e.g. the CSEW interviews take an average of 48 minutes per interview to complete)	Only snapshots taken at one moment in time, and so they fail to capture the dynamic changing nature of social life
The interviewer can explain the aims and objectives of the research, clarify instructions and generally make sure that informed consent has been granted	Interpretivists note that there is often a gap between what people say they do and what they actually do – they may not put their prejudices into action or they may be unaware that they behave in certain ways
Better response rates than postal questionnaires, as the interviewer can return if the respondent is not at home	All interviews are interactions, so there is the danger of interview bias in that the interviewee will feel that he or she lacks power or status compared to the interviewer, and may feel threatened by the research. Anxiety about how their responses are used may result in a lack of openness and cooperation from interviewees, thus undermining validity
Regarded as scientific *and* reliable by positivist sociologists because they are standardized measuring instruments; interviewers can be trained to conduct each interview in exactly the same way (e.g. same questions, order, wording and tone of voice), and so should produce similar data	Responses may lack validity because the interviewee responds in a socially desirable way. They may try to manage or manipulate the interviewer's impression of them by giving untruthful or partial answers, therefore increasing the potential for invalid data

Table 7
Advantages and disadvantages of structured interviews

Secondary data – official statistics

Positivists are keen on some types of secondary data, such as official statistics collected by government agencies. The most commonly available sources of official statistics are those from the Census – a questionnaire survey that is conducted every 10 years on the whole population. Official statistics have a number of strengths and weaknesses.

Official statistics – strengths

- easy and cheap to access, involving little effort on the part of the sociologist
- contemporary (e.g. the 2016 crime statistics will be published in 2017)
- usually collected in a standardized, systematic and scientific way (e.g. registration data on birth, marriage, divorce and death is highly reliable and valid, because it is the outcome of longstanding, systematic procedures)
- allow us to make comparisons between groups (e.g. the Census covers the whole UK population at the same time and asks everyone the same questions, making it easy to compare different groups and regions)
- trends over a period of time can be observed easily (e.g. sociologists might notice that there is less property crime and more violent crime in 2017 compared with 2016)
- generally regarded as representative, as they have been produced by large-scale studies, often covering the whole population

Official statistics – weaknesses

- may not present a complete picture of whatever the sociologist is studying (e.g. the government does not collect statistics relating to the socio-economic background or employment status of people who have been arrested, prosecuted or convicted and sent to prison)
- open to political abuse (e.g. they can be manipulated or 'massaged' by governments for political advantage)
- socially constructed (i.e. they are often the end result of someone making a decision that a particular set of activities needs to be recorded and that statistics need to be collected in a particular way – for example, statistics on ethnic minority crime may tell us more about institutional racism in the police or the stereotypical decisions by some police officers to stop black people more frequently than white people)
- they tell us very little about the human stories or interpretations that underpin them (e.g. crime and prison statistics tell us little about *why* people commit crime or what it feels like to be sent to prison)
- may be based on operational definitions, with which sociologists would not agree (e.g. the government often changes definitions of serious drug offences)
- Marxists argue that their ideological function is to conceal or distort reality and keep the capitalist class in power – e.g. the official crime statistics (OCS) create the impression that street crime committed by the working class is the main criminal problem in the UK, but Marxists argue that such statistics serve to distract society from white-collar, corporate and state crime

Examiners' notes

Make sure you give examples of interview bias. Illustrate how power or status differences between the interviewer and interviewees might undermine the validity of the research data. For example, if interviewees are teenagers, it might be useful to employ young rather than middle-aged interviewers; if the sample are female, they may be put off by male interviewers; black and Asian inerviewees might be reluctant to discuss their experiences of racism with white interviewers.

Essential notes

Sociologists often use official statistics to work out the extent of a social problem so that primary research can be designed to uncover explanations. Criminologists often use the criminal statistics to work out which groups are more likely to commit crime. Durkheim used 19th-century official statistics to study suicide.

Examiners' notes

Use the interpretivist arguments regarding the social construction of the criminal statistics to illustrate in depth the weaknesses of this type of secondary data.

The use of sampling in social research

Sociologists who use the questionnaire or structured interview survey to test a hypothesis need to think about the research population they are studying and how it should be sampled:

The research population

For example, if the sociologist is interested in the relationship between ethnicity and being the victim of racial attacks, decisions must be made about which ethnic minority groups will be focused on and whether the white population will also be studied, possibly as a point of comparison.

The sample

It is usually too expensive and time-consuming to ask everyone in the research population to take part in the research. Most researchers select a sample that is representative – a typical cross-section – of the population they are interested in. With a representative sample, it is possible to **generalize** to the wider research population – what is true of the sample should be true of the research population as a whole.

Two main sampling techniques are used to choose samples of people to take part in social research. They are:

- **random sampling**
- **non-random** sampling.

Random sampling

A simple random sample involves selecting names randomly from a list or **sampling frame**. Using this technique, every member of the research population has an equal chance to be included in the sample, so that those chosen are likely to be a cross-section of the population.

Various types of sampling frames can be used:

- the Electoral Register (that is, a list of people over 18 years, who are registered to vote)
- the Postcode Address File
- the telephone directory
- school attendance registers
- patient records of general practitioners (GPs).

All sampling frames are unsatisfactory in some respect – they are often out of date; some groups may be over-represented, while others may not be included.

Different types of random sampling techniques

A simple random sample does not guarantee a representative sample – the researcher may, for example, end up selecting too many young people or too many males. Thus, to produce representative samples, sociologists have developed three variations on the random sample.

- **Systematic sampling** involves randomly choosing a number between 1 and 10, say '7', and then picking out every 10th number from that number – 7, 17, 27, 37 … – on the list until the sample is complete. This does not always guarantee a representative sample, but the larger the sample, the more likely it is to be reasonably representative and the less likely it is to be biased.

- **Stratified sampling** is the most common form of random sampling used in sociological research. It involves dividing the research population into a number of sampling frames – for example, by gender, age, ethnicity and social class – which represent their proportion in the research population, and then randomly selecting, say, every 10th name until the required number is reached for each sub-sample.
- **Cluster sampling** is often used when no specific list of people is available. The researcher uses a map to randomly select a couple of areas, and then streets within those areas. The researcher then randomly targets a further sample of people or households within the streets.

Non-random sampling methods

- **Quota sampling** is often used by market research companies to target people in the street to talk about consumer products. The researcher is told by his or her company how many participants are needed in each category and goes looking for them, usually in a city centre. This sort of sampling technique is often used by television news companies and newspapers to find out people's voting preferences before an election.
- **Purposive sampling** involves researchers choosing individuals or cases that fit the nature of the research. For example, a researcher might purposely visit a church because he or she needs to interview religious people.
- **Snowball sampling** is used mainly when it is difficult to gain access to a particular group of people because there is no sampling frame available or because they engage in deviant or illegal activities, which are normally done in isolation or in secret. This sampling technique involves finding and interviewing a person who fits the research criteria and then asking her or him to suggest someone else who might be willing to be interviewed. The sample can grow as large as the researcher wants. Martin A. Plant (1975) used this type of sampling technique in his study of cannabis use. However, this technique may not produce a representative sample, as the type of people who volunteer may differ in important respects from those who do not volunteer.

All sampling is a compromise between representativeness and practicality, and researchers often have to make do with samples that are not fully representative.

Examiners' notes

Note that positivist survey research such as the CSEW is most likely to use random sampling techniques, whereas interpretivist **qualitative research** is more likely to use non-random sampling techniques.

Interpretivists reject the positivist view that human behaviour is the product of social laws over which people have no control. They argue that we are not the puppets of society – rather, we are the architects of society. Without people, society simply would not exist. Interpretivists also reject the view that humans can be treated like objects in much the same way as things in the natural world.

Interpretivists point out that people are active, conscious beings who act with intention and purpose. They are not propelled against their will to take certain predetermined or predictable courses of action. Instead, they make choices based on free will.

Interpretivists argue that society is the sum of people choosing to come together in social groups – known as 'social interaction'. Interpretivists point out that, when people interact, they are constantly interpreting, or giving meaning to, their own behaviour and that of others. Interpretivists therefore argue that through these interactions and interpretations people socially construct society. In this sense, they actively create and control their own social realities rather than being passively shaped by social factors over which they have no control. For example, a family is not just a group of people with a biological relationship, they are a group of people who interpret themselves as a family and interact accordingly.

Interpretivists argue that, in order to understand social behaviour (and therefore society), it is essential to discover and understand the meanings or interpretations that underpin people's actions. Interpretivist sociologists therefore stress the concept of validity – seeing the world as it really is. They argue that sociologists need to adopt sociological research methods that are ethnographic – methods that access people's natural everyday environment. Such methods should get inside people's heads in order to see the social world through the eyes of those being studied. This is called *verstehen* or empathetic understanding.

Key study

J. Maxwell Atkinson's study of coroners

Atkinson is critical of Durkheim's use of official statistics. He argues that suicide rates are not social facts, as Durkheim argued. Rather, suicide rates are socially constructed because they are the end product of a complex set of interactions and interpretations involving victims, doctors, friends and relatives of the deceased and, significantly, coroners.

Atkinson specifically focuses on the role of coroners. These are legal officers whose function is to investigate suspicious death. Atkinson notes that officially a death is not a suicide until it has been labelled as such by a coroner's court.

When investigating suspicious death, coroners in the UK can use five possible verdicts. If the cause of death is not due to natural causes, the coroner may conclude that death was caused by misadventure (accidental death), homicide or suicide. The 'open' verdict is used if evidence is insufficient to allow him or her to come to a definite conclusion. A coroner will only bring in a suicide verdict if he or she is convinced that the deceased intended to die.

Atkinson observed coroner's courts and interviewed coroners. He found that they aim to uncover suicidal intent (intention to die) by looking for primary and secondary suicidal cues. Primary cues include suicide notes, mode of death and location of death. However, these are not clear indicators of intent to die. Only a minority of suicides leave notes, many of which are vague, ambiguous in content and open to interpretation. Some types or modes of deaths are clearly suicidal – for example, hanging – but others, particularly drug overdoses, are not clear-cut – for example, if the peron was drunk, it could be an accidental overdose. Some locations are notorious suicide spots and so a death in a particular place may be a clue that the person intended to die. However, Atkinson concludes that primary cues in themselves are insufficient to prove suicidal intent.

The coroner requires extra evidence in the form of secondary cues, which involve the coroner looking for signs of intent in the deceased's life history and state of mind prior to death. Atkinson also argues that dominant **cultural meanings** associated with suicide (for example, that it is it is caused by despair and great unhappiness) also influence coroners.

Atkinson also notes that details of the deceased's life history or state of mind (and therefore whether they are unhappy or not) often come from negotiation with relatives, who may attempt to influence the coroner's verdict.

In conclusion, then, Atkinson suggests that we cannot take suicide statistics at face value, as Durkheim did. Sociologists must look at the way suicide statistics are socially constructed. It may be that the official suicide statistics tell us more about the ways particular deaths are interpreted by coroners than they tell us about the causes of suicide.

Interpretivist sociologists prefer research methods such as unstructured interviews, which allow people to talk at length about how they feel, and participant observation (observing behaviour by joining in their everyday activities), as these methods produce qualitative data – concerned with motives, feelings and experiences that give us first-hand insight into how people interpret the world around them. Interpretivists reject methods such as questionnaires, which they say are artificial and are unlikely to produce data that tell us how people really feel.

Field or social experiments

Interpretivists reject the use of laboratory experiments, because they argue that human beings are fundamentally different from the plants, rocks and other natural phenomena that natural scientists study. Unlike these objects, we have free will and choice. Our behaviour is not 'caused'

☞ **This topic continues on the next six pages**

Examiners' notes

Atkinson used a social experiment to compare British and Danish coroners. Make sure you are able to clearly differentiate this type of experiment from other types. Also be aware of its strengths and weaknesses as a method.

by external forces, so it cannot be explained in terms of cause and effect statements, as positivists believe.

However, interpretivists have conducted social experiments in naturally occurring settings. These **field experiments** aim to examine the way people behave in everyday, small social groups. The sociologist manipulates one particular variable, or influence, and observes the reactions of the individual or group who are being studied (and who are often not aware that a social experiment is taking place). These experiments differ from conventional laboratory experiments in that control groups are not always apparent – it is assumed that the control group is made up of similar groups who are not taking part in the experiment.

Essential notes

In the field of criminology, field experiments are often used to test the effectiveness of social policies, such as crime prevention programmes or prisoner rehabilitation, by comparing situations where a policy is being implemented with situations where it is not.

> **Key study**
>
> **Rosenthal and Jacobson – Pygmalion in the classroom**
>
> Robert Rosenthal and Lenore Jacobson (1968) manipulated teachers' expectations about students by giving them misleading information about students' abilities in order to discover what effects this would have on students' achievements.

Field experiments allow the sociologist to unravel the often hidden processes and rules of day-to-day social life, as they enable the researcher to get close to people's interpretations of everyday experiences. However, field experiments have been criticized because:

- There is often a trade-off between naturalism and control – the more natural and realistic the situation, the less control the sociologist has over variables.
- Such experiments may be unethical because they have not gained the informed consent of the participants and they often involve deception. However, interpretivist sociologists argue that deception rarely involves harm being done and that the data generated by the experiment often benefits society.
- There is a danger of a Hawthorne effect being created. For example, if a field experiment were to be conducted in a prison, any change to everyday procedures might be noticed by prisoners and guards, so their behaviour might change because of the experiment.

Unstructured interviews

Essential notes

Unstructured interviews are useful in revealing the truth beneath the surface, because they ask individuals open-ended questions about their specific experiences rather than asking the whole sample the same questions and getting them to choose responses from the same set of answers.

An unstructured interview is like a guided conversation, in which the talk is informal but the researcher plays an active role, in that he or she manages the questions to ensure that the participant sticks to the subject of the research. The interviewer in this situation usually has a list of topics to discuss rather than an interview schedule or questionnaire. A skilful interviewer will flexibly follow up ideas, probe responses and investigate motives and feelings in ways a questionnaire can never do.

Interpretivist sociologists are keen on unstructured interviews, because they are concerned with understanding the meanings or interpretations that underpin social life. They believe that unstructured interviews bring about validity through involvement, meaning that valid qualitative data can only be obtained by getting close to people's experiences and ways of thinking. The way an unstructured interview is organized stresses that what the interviewee says or thinks is the central issue – the respondent is placed at the centre of the research. By developing trust and **rapport** with the interviewee, the researcher can visualize his or her points of view – which is important, because it can give insight into why he or she acts in a certain way.

Unstructured interviews have a number of strengths and weaknesses.

Unstructured interviews – strengths

- allow researchers to build up and modify their hypothesis during the course of the research, as new and important insights come about, either because the interviewee trusts the researcher or because the flexible nature of the interview results in unexpected information being uncovered
- Well-trained interviewers should be sensitive to and be able to avoid problems such as interview bias and impression management associated with structured interviews.
- some sociologists use them as a starting point to develop their initial ideas, before using more structured methods such as questionnaires
- allow the interviewer to make sure that he or she shares the same meaning as the interviewee about a particular issue, thus increasing validity
- seen as particularly suited to researching sensitive groups (i.e. people who might be suspicious of or hostile to outsiders – such as deviants or criminals)
- provide richer, more vivid and more qualitative data – the data collected often speaks for itself in the form of extensive quotations from those being interviewed

Unstructured interviews – weaknesses

- regarded as unreliable by positivists because they cannot be replicated and their results verified by another sociologist
- may lack objectivity because the researcher has a personal relationship with the interviewee
- practically speaking, the final research cannot contain all the information gathered and, often, the interviewer will select aspects of the interview transcript that fit the hypothesis – such selectivity may reflect the ideological biases of the researcher
- data is difficult to analyse and categorize because of the sheer volume of material in the respondent's own words
- exceptionally time-consuming to conduct and transcribe
- expensive, as training must be thorough and specialized – interviewers need to be trained in interpersonal skills so that they establish good relationships with interviewees
- all interviews are interactions and there is always the danger that the interviewee will feel that they lack power or status compared to the interviewer (although the interviewer should be trained to look out for, and should be skilled enough to avoid, this problem)

Essential notes

People conducting unstructured interviews should have similar social characteristics to those being interviewed, to minimize interview bias and to increase the possibility of trust.

Essential notes

Some people may be defensive and distrustful of sociological research. The higher level of trust and rapport associated with unstructured interviews can help to overcome this barrier.

Essential notes

Unstructured interviews may be ethically problematic, as they may reveal 'guilty knowledge' – the sociologist becomes aware of crimes the respondent has committed or intends to commit. This begs the question – should the researcher inform the police?

Examiners' notes

Make sure you give examples of possible interview bias. Use social class, gender, ethnicity or age to illustrate how power or status differences might undermine the validity of the research data.

Personal documents

Some interpretivists use a form of secondary data known as personal or expressive documents, made up of diaries, letters and autobiographies. These can be historical or contemporary, and can provide a sociologist with a rich source of qualitative data about, for example, experiences, feelings, attitudes, emotions and motives for behaviour. Sociologists are drawn to this type of data because they are a free or economical source of information, already having been gathered. They may also be used when no other source of data exists. For example, sociologists might not be able to gain access to criminal gangs, but the diary or autobiography of a gang member may give us important insights into criminal behaviour.

Interpretivists like documents. They believe documents can give the researcher a valid picture of people's world-view and the meaning they apply to their actions. Documents enable sociologists to get close to people's reality. For example, suicide notes can be taken to be the final thoughts of the individual committing suicide. Personal documents are particularly useful for giving insight into how people behaved in the past.

However, personal documents are often very subjective and biased, in that the writer usually wants to justify his or her actions. There may also be doubts about the **authenticity** of the document – letters and diaries can be forged. A document may lack **credibility** if it was written long after the events it describes, when key details might have been forgotten.

Positivists are not keen on documents, because they regard this type of data as unreliable – it cannot be checked for accuracy by the sociologist. Documents are not standardized. For example, every person's diary is unique, even when they record the same events. Finally, the people who write personal documents may not be representative – not all sections of society keep diaries describing their behaviour. The nature of criminal activity means that criminals are less likely than other social groups to leave personal records that incriminate them and perhaps lead to their prosecution.

Key study

Steve Taylor and deaths on the London Underground

Research by Steve Taylor (1982), based on interviews with coroners and their officers and observation of inquests, found that coroners see breakdowns in personal relationships, unemployment, history of both mental and physical illness and coming from a broken home as important aspects of unhappiness.

Taylor investigated 32 deaths under London Underground trains in 1982, where the mode and scene of death were identical and no suicide notes were left. Only 17 of these were eventually labelled as suicide. On observation of the inquests, Taylor concluded that suicide verdicts were not returned on the other 15 because relatives influenced the coroner's interpretation of secondary cues.

Observation

Interpretivist sociologists argue that observation gives first-hand insight into how people interpret the social world around them. It allows sociologists to record behaviour by observing people's actions on a daily basis. Consequently, they see the world through the eyes of the group they are observing.

Essentially, there are two types of observation.

1. Non-participant or direct observation

This has been used extensively in the field of criminal justice and usually involves the researcher observing an activity such as police–suspect interaction. The researcher plays no active role. For example, Smith and Grey went out on the beat with London Metropolitan Police officers, while Cicourel sat in the back of patrol cars and observed LA police officers interact with suspects and members of the general public.

2. Participant observation

This is the most common type of observation and involves sociologists immersing themselves in the lifestyle of the group they wish to study. Sociological observers participate in the same activities as the group being researched and observe their everyday lives.

The aim of participant observation is to understand what is happening from the point of view of those involved and to understand the meaning that they give to their situation. The research, then, is ethnographic – conducted in the natural environment of the group being studied. This type of research may take many months and even years to complete.

Participant observation can be either:

- overt, when the researcher joins in the activities of a group but some or all of the group know his or her identity

  or
- covert, when the researcher conceals the fact that she or he is doing research, and pretends to be a member of the group.

It can be very difficult to gain entry to a group, though some groups are easier to enter than others. For example, joining a football crowd is likely to be easier than joining a criminal gang.

A skilled researcher will focus on 'looking and listening', and going with the flow of social life once he or she has gained entry to a group, and will not try to force the pace or interfere with or disrupt 'normality'. Instead, the skilled researcher will blend into the background until he or she has gained the group's trust and his or her presence is taken for granted. Much of participant observation, therefore, involves 'hanging around'.

Key study

Sudhir Venkatesh

Sudhir Venkatesh spent seven years living with poor families inside one of Chicago's worst housing projects and hanging out with gang

Essential notes

Both J. Maxwell Atkinson and Steve Taylor used this type of observation to observe coroners in action at inquests.

Examiners' notes

Make sure you are able to illustrate how this type of observation works in practice, with reference to particular studies.

Examiners' notes

Make sure you are able to illustrate how participant observation works in practice, with reference to particular studies.

Essential notes

Sharing the same or similar characteristics to the group being researched is crucial to the success of the research. For example, Venkatesh's relative youth worked in his favour.

members of a crack-dealing gang called the Black Kings in the late 1990s. Venkatesh was able to establish a trusting friendship with JT, the leader of the Black Kings, who showed him how the gang operated on a daily basis within the project. Venkatesh notes that 'JT seemed to appreciate having the ear of an outsider who would listen for hours to his tales of bravado and managerial prowess'. Venkatesh's relationship with JT meant that Venkatesh was able to gain access to areas of gang life that are not usually accessible to sociologists (for example, he witnessed violence being used to discipline gang members). Venkatesh observed that his relationship with JT meant he was able to gain insights into how gang members saw themselves and justified their behaviour, which was unlikely to be obtained via questionnaires or interviews. For example, JT often expressed how hard it was to manage the gang, to keep the drug economy running smoothly and to deal with the law-abiding tenants, who saw him as an adversary. The research culminated in a remarkable research opportunity when JT invited Venkatesh to become the 'gang leader for a day'.

Essential notes

Observation can be supplemented with asking questions, although if the researcher is conducting covert research, this might arouse suspicion and mistrust. Observers sometimes develop special relationships with key people within groups, who can clarify the motives for particular types of behaviour – for example, Venkatesh was able to question JT to cross-check his interpretation of events.

Essential notes

In a classic participant observation study, William Whyte noted: 'As I sat and listened, I learned the answers to questions that I would not have had the sense to ask if I had been getting my information solely on an interviewing basis.'

Participant observation has a number of strengths and weaknesses.

Participant observation – strengths

- the researcher is placed in exactly the same situation as the group under study and large amounts of qualitative data are generated, giving the sociologist a feel for what it is like to be a member of the group. This allows the sociologist to achieve a state of 'verstehen' or empathetic understanding – the sociologist sees the world through the eyes of the group being studied which increases the validity of the data.
- what people say and what they actually do can be very different and people are often unaware that they are acting in a certain way (i.e. in observation studies, the sociologist can see what people really do, so is more likely to be able to record the truth, so validity is high)
- it can generate new ideas and lead to new insights (i.e. the sociologist might see things which inspire ideas that they would not have had if they had been using solely questionnaires and/or interviews) – for example, would a gang leader have admitted that they found their job 'hard' if Venkatesh had been using a positivist research method?
- hypotheses can be changed or developed as the research progresses or as new situations are encountered, allowing an understanding of how changes in attitudes and behaviour take place over months and years

Participant observation – weaknesses

- presence of observer may result in the group acting less naturally because they are aware of being observed and studied, though covert observation is less likely to lead to this effect
- some observers can get too close or attached to 'their' group and consequently observations become biased (e.g. the observer may become overly sympathetic towards the group and 'go native', losing detachment and objectivity) – Venkatesh was accused of this

- there is no way of knowing if the researcher's findings are true or not, since it is impossible to repeat the research and verify the data, so reliability is low; however, the longitudinal character of participant observation studies means that the same behaviour was likely to be observed several times
- the findings are merely the observer's view of things, and he or she may use personal choice to select facts worth recording, which may match their own values and prejudices.
- the sociologist must make value judgements in selecting what to include and what to omit from their final account, leaving a potential for bias, because the sociologist may select aspects of the observation that fit his or her research hypothesis
- some sociologists object to this method because it lacks ethical consideration for those being researched especially if the research is covert. Laud Humphreys argues that some situations, particularly the study of deviant behaviour, will always have to involve some degree of deception to ensure validity. For example, it may involve the sociologist being forced to break the law in order to gain or retain the trust of the group, or to protect his or her cover. Humphreys therefore suggests that the situation determines the ethical approach – situational ethics means that sometimes the potential research findings are so important that ethical considerations need to be suspended
- observation produces large amounts of qualitative data, which is difficult to analyse and categorize.

Mixing methods

Triangulation involves the use of more than one research method or source of data in the course of a single study. A researcher can use more than one primary source and also use secondary data. Positivists promote the use of exclusively quantitative sources, whereas interpretivists prefer qualitative sources. In practice, many studies combine both types of sources and the triangulation of methods is common.

Types of triangulation

Martyn Hammersley (1996) distinguishes three ways of combining methods:

1. Triangulation – findings are cross-checked using a variety of methods; for example, interviews are used to check the responses made in questionnaires.
2. **Facilitation** – one method is used to assist or develop the use of another method; for example, in-depth unstructured interviews might be used to help devise closed questions and their coded responses for questionnaires.
3. **Complementarity** – different methods are combined to dovetail different aspects of an investigation; for example, questionnaires might be used to discover overall statistical patterns and participant observation might be used to reveal the reasons for these patterns.

Essential notes

This observer or Hawthorne effect can seriously undermine the validity of the research data. For example, the gang leader 'Doc' in William Whyte's research announced that he used to do things on instinct but now behaved differently because he felt he had to justify his actions to Whyte.

Essential notes

Paul Rock suggests that if the group a sociologist is observing no longer surprises or shocks the observer, the researcher has lost his or her objectivity and the research should end. Rock argues that a good observer should always be critical of the group they are studying.

Examiners' notes

Make sure you can identify at least three strengths and three weaknesses of covert participant observation compared to the more common overt version.

Examiners' notes

Triangulation may generate a small question in its own right but it is also useful for concluding discussions about any single method. To help you write conclusions in research method essays, use this section to point out that each method can be complemented with other methods, which provide different types of data or help to fill in the gaps.

Essential notes

Positivists regard sociological methods such as the social survey, the structured interview and official statistics as scientific.

Examiners' notes

The notion of whether sociology is a science is a popular choice for Theory and Method questions. Positivists believe that the logic and methods of the natural sciences are best suited to the study of the social sciences. Essay titles are often a variation on this statement.

During the 19th century, the natural sciences proved successful in taking control of nature and producing technology that improved people's living standards. Positivist sociologists such as Durkheim and Marx felt they could copy the success of science and produce a science of society, which could be used to eradicate problems such as poverty, injustice and conflict. Positivists believe that sociology is a science and that sociologists should seek to uncover the social laws that they believe underpin human behaviour by adopting the logic and methods of the natural sciences.

Positivist science is based on the **hypothetico-deductive model**, which stresses that scientific discovery should go through a number of logical stages:

Stage 1: An observation is made of social phenomena.

Stage 2: A hypothesis explaining the phenomena is formulated.

Stage 3: Evidence is collected in a systematic, objective and reliable fashion to deduce whether the hypothesis is true or false.

Stage 4: If sufficient data support the hypothesis, it becomes a theory and eventually a scientific or social law.

However, the positivist view of science and scientific method has been subjected to severe criticism over the years. Much of this critique has stemmed from the observation that positivist sociological research has not yet discovered any 'scientific' laws, despite a century of effort.

Karl Popper – philosopher of science

However, philosophers of science such as Karl Popper have questioned the logic of the positivist hypothetico-deductive approach to doing science because the emphasis in positivist research is on looking for evidence that confirms the hypothesis. Popper suggested that scientists should look for evidence that proves the hypothesis absolutely wrong and forces them to look elsewhere.

Popper claimed that there is no such thing as 'objective truth' that can be discovered and documented. At best, we can only achieve partial truth, because all knowledge is provisional or temporary. This is because, no matter how many times an experiment is conducted or a phenomenon is observed, the scientist can never be certain that the same results will be obtained in the future.

Popper illustrated this idea by using the hypothesis 'Swans are always white'. He notes that many positivist scientists would be content to confirm this hypothesis after 999 observations of white swans. The notion that 'all swans are white' would become a scientific fact and it is unlikely that further observations would be conducted. However, Popper notes that this is bad science, because there is always the possibility that a black swan will appear and prove this 'fact' wrong. Popper suggested that scientist need to look for the 'black swan' straight away. In other words, scientists should set out to refute their hypotheses, i.e. to prove them wrong rather than just collect evidence that supports the hypothesis.

Popper argues that we can never be conclusively right, we can only be conclusively wrong. No amount of evidence in support of one hypothesis can ever prove that hypothesis right, whereas a single piece of evidence that contradicts the hypothesis proves it absolutely wrong. Referring to his swan example, all the positivist scientist can say with any confidence is 'The swans observed *so far* are white.'

Popper argues that good science is about being rigorously sceptical and he proposed that scientific research methods should be based on the '**principle of falsification**', that is, instead of looking for evidence to prove a hypothesis right, scientists should look for evidence that proves it wrong or false. Popper argues that scientific knowledge is that which survives after rigorous testing – this knowledge can be tentatively accepted as close to the truth, although the possibility that one day contradictory evidence might appear denies it the status of real scientific truth.

Popper was sceptical about the scientific status of sociology, because he argued that it was too theoretical and not engaged in enough testing or research. However, although this was probably true at the time Popper was writing, modern sociology has engaged extensively in the research process in ways that stress that nothing should ever be taken on trust or at face value and that evidence should be subjected to the most rigorous critical examination.

Evaluation of Karl Popper

Paul Feyerabend is critical of positivists and of Popper because both portray the scientific method as being a coldly logical and rational process. However, Feyerabend suggests that what scientists say they do is often different from what they actually do in practice. He claims there is no such thing as a scientific method that is good for all times and in all places. Instead, he argues that in reality there is no logic to science – the rule seems to be 'anything goes'; individual scientists follow their own rules, which often do not resemble textbook models.

Abraham Kaplan agrees with Feyerabend and points out that many scientific discoveries are made almost by accident, and that inspired guesses, imagination and luck play a crucial role in scientific research. Moreover, many scientists make false starts or collect data that takes them up blind alleys before they get back on track. Cheating is fairly common in science, mainly because scientists are heavily biased toward proving their own theories right. There is not much chance of being caught, as little attempt is made to replicate and verify the work of other scientists – there is no prestige in repeating someone else's work. Reliability in this sense is over-rated.

Scientific logic is imposed afterwards, during the writing-up process. Its function is to mystify scientific knowledge and to convince ordinary people that scientists deserve greater status and rewards because only scientists understand the logic of scientific enquiry.

Essential notes

Popper was particularly critical of Marxism, which he dismissed as unscientifc because it makes predictions about the future, which he argued cannot be refuted.

This topic continues on the next two pages

Scientific Realism

Scientific Realists such as Andrew Sayer argue that many sciences theorize about the existence of phenomena which are difficult or impossible to observe, detect and therefore predict.

Realists are interested in the so-called **open sciences** – those concerned with the study of things we cannot see or sense directly – such as seismology, meteorology, astronomy and some schools of physics such as cosmology. Sayer notes that open sciences are often unable to predict how the phenomena they are studying will behave. For example, seismologists cannot predict precisely when and where an earthquake will occur, so controlling variables is virtually impossible.

From a Realist position, sociology can be seen as scientific because it is largely concerned with developing models of underlying social structures and processes, which are largely unobservable but can be evaluated and modified by examining their effects. For example, social class as a social and economic force cannot be observed directly but its effects on social behaviour, such as educational behaviour, and on aspects of health, such as life expectancy and death rates, can be measured. So, in this sense, sociology could be classed as an open science.

Science and paradigms

Thomas Kuhn argues that scientists are not as open-minded as positivists claim. He rejects the idea that scientists are constantly making and testing hypotheses, arguing instead that they are concerned mainly with solving problems defined as important by earlier influential scientists. In other words, scientists usually work within a set of assumptions, left by an earlier generation of scientists, about what the natural world is like. Scientists take these assumptions as being correct, rather than questioning them. Kuhn calls this set of assumptions **paradigms** and argues that they shape and define scientists' views of the world – telling them what their priorities should be, what counts as legitimate evidence, how to approach specific problems and what scientific method to adopt.

Kuhn suggests that scientific progress only occurs because, as time passes, more and more evidence which does not fit the paradigm appears. At first, it is ignored or explained away, but eventually it becomes so numerous that the dominant paradigm loses credibility and is overthrown in a 'scientific revolution'. A new paradigm is established, and normal science resumes. Kuhn sees science as a body of knowledge constructed and created by scientists working within a specific paradigmatic context. So, scientific method is not free to wander as it wishes – it is constrained by accepted assumptions about how the world is organized.

Using Kuhn's definition of science, sociology is probably not scientific because it is doubtful that there has been one paradigm dominant at any one time within the discipline of sociology. Sociology has long been characterized by competing theoretical perspectives and, even within these, there is intense disagreement.

Interpretivism and science

Interpretivist sociology is sceptical about positivist sociology's claim to scientific status and has generally taken an anti-positivist position. Interpretivists do not believe sociology is scientific. They argue that the logic and methods of the natural sciences are unsuitable for sociology because its subject matter – humans – are active conscious beings, who are aware of what is going on around them and who constantly make choices about how to act and react.

Interpretivists reject the positivist notion that society is the product of social laws, so scientific procedures are needed to uncover these. Interpretivists argue that the focus of sociological research should be the interpretations or meanings that people bring to the social interactions that make up society.

Interpretivists argue for the adoption of research methods that help reveal the meanings that lie behind everyday social action. Mainly, they support the use of qualitative ethnographic methods, which focus on people in their everyday natural context and place emphasis upon *verstehen* (empathy with research subjects) and validity – the reality of those being studied. Positivist scientific methods are criticized and rejected by interpretivists, as, inevitably, they result in the sociologists' views of the world being imposed on the research subjects.

Postmodernism and science

Postmodernists reject the view that there exists any absolute and universal truth and knowledge. Therefore, they reject science as the embodiment of this idea. Postmodernists are especially critical of science because it claims to be objective. However, postmodernists argue that scientific knowledge is subjective and reflects the values of powerful Western interest groups. The rules of science such as logic and rationality are merely ways in which powerful people attempt to control ways of thinking.

Postmodernists argue that scientific truth and certainty are illusions constructed by Western academics. They argue that science has no more authority than other subjective versions of events. Postmodernists believe positivist sociology should abandon its search for ultimate truth, because no such thing exists. They support a more pluralistic approach to scientific enquiry. They also prefer to use a range of research techniques to capture and analyse the many different interpretations of reality that postmodernists claim are found in postmodern society.

Essential notes

Some sociologists claim that sociology exists in a permanent state of revolution, whereas others claim sociology is in a pre-paradigmatic state, meaning that a single paradigm has yet to be accepted.

Essential notes

Interpretivist sociologists do not reject scientific principles altogether. They argue that reliability can still be achieved, but in different ways from those proposed by positivists. For example, observation data can be verified by checking and rechecking what has been observed and by supplementing observations with informal conversations with those being studied.

Examiners' notes

Exam questions on this topic usually focus on evaluating the idea that sociology can and should model itself on the natural sciences. Responses to this type of question should focus on how science is defined. Positivist definitions generally conflict with those of Popper, Kuhn and interpretivism.

Value-free sociology

During the 19th century, Auguste Comte believed that sociology should be a **prescriptive** science of society. In his view, the purpose of sociology was to propose remedies for social and moral problems. This approach influenced the early poverty studies of Charles Booth and Seebohm Rowntree, which described the extent of poverty in the East End of London and York respectively and proposed remedies for its eradication.

However, in the early 20th century, positivist sociologists decided that it was not the sociologists' job to fix society. Instead, they argued, the role of sociology was to document social processes and problems in an objective way. It was the role of the social policy makers (such as politicians and civil servants) to act on sociological findings.

Positivists stressed 'objectivity through neutrality' – that sociologists should be the impartial and trustworthy pursuers of truth, so aiming only to see facts as they are, not as they might wish to see them. In this sense, sociologists aimed to be **value free** – to not let personal prejudices, tastes and beliefs influence their research methods or findings. They saw their job as simply to establish the truth about people's behaviour, not to praise or condemn it.

The idea that sociology should be value free became especially popular with functionalist sociologists in the USA, who in the post-war period were employed heavily by the state to advise the US Army as well as by large corporations who were interested in research that might improve the profitability of how they organized their factories and offices.

The critique of value freedom

- Max Weber rejected the notion of value freedom. He argued that scientists and sociologists are also human, and citizens, and should not avoid the moral and political issues raised by their work by hiding behind words such as 'objectivity' or 'value freedom'. They must take moral responsibility for the harm their research might do.
- Alvin Gouldner agreed and argued that, by the 1950s, American positivist sociologists had become 'spiritless technicians' who rarely questioned or criticized their paymasters.

Five broad criticisms of the concept of value freedom

1. Studies done by sociologists depend on those with power and funding, especially the government and large corporations, making value judgements about what is interesting and worthwhile. For example, corporate businesses have funded a huge amount of research in the USA aimed at improving worker productivity. Moreover, powerful groups have the power to resist sociological research. It is a fact that there have been many studies of the poor and the working class but relatively few studies of wealthy or powerful institutions such as public schools. Roger Gomm notes that value freedom often depends on who controls the values.
2. The personal values of sociologists may influence the choice of research topic, as they may wish to further their careers and reputations. Some sociologists censor themselves for fear that being

too outspoken will harm their career prospects or even cost them their job. Sociologists in university departments are also likely to be under pressure from universities to publish research, regardless of its quality or usefulness.

3. Derek Phillips points out that data collection is itself a social process, so we can expect bias and invalidity to arise from the effects of interaction with research subjects. For example, in questionnaires and structured interviews, the sociologist has already decided which experiences of the subjects of research are important, by designing specific questions and providing a limited choice of response boxes to tick. By doing this, the sociologist imposes his or her values on the research subjects.

   • A major problem with interviews is the interview effect, in which interviewees may feel threatened by status differences between themselves and the interviewers. One effect is the **social desirability effect** – the interviewees work out the value position of the interviewers and provide the answers the interviewers are looking for, to please them.

   • Participant observation may result in the sociological observer **going native**. This means that he or she becomes too friendly with the people being observed, thus losing the ability to be objective and critical about the group's behaviour. Some observers, notably Sudhir Venkatesh, get so involved with a group that they engage in deviant behaviour.

   • There is often a link between the kinds of methods sociologists prefer and their value stance. For example, **interpretivists**' preference for qualitative methods fits with their desire to empathize with the underdog, since such methods give them access to the actor's meanings and world-view (see pp 88–91). Functionalists tend to take the side of the 'establishment' and see things from the viewpoint of those in authority. This fits well with their uncritical acceptance of official government-produced statistics. Interactionists and functionalists can be accused of selecting methods that produce facts that reflect their values and outlook.

4. Alvin Gouldner argues that value-free sociology is a myth, as sociology is made up of socially organized knowledge, characterized by, for example, collective social values and prejudices. It is like this because sociologists are members of society and therefore cannot escape the influence of its culture and institutions. Gouldner argues that all researchers possess **domain assumptions** – a world-view which is the result of socialization into a certain culture. As a result, most American and European sociology reflects Western, capitalist and patriarchal values.

   Gomm also notes that doing sociology is a social activity carried out by real people in a world characterized by conflicts of interest between different social groups. Therefore, any research must inevitably take one side or the other, whether the researcher admits this or not. Sociological research, according to Gomm, reflects ideological beliefs.

Essential notes

Not all sociologists will be influenced by who is paying their salaries. The Sociology Department of Leicester University was given £100,000 by the Conservative government in the 1980s to investigate football hooliganism. Leicester's findings based upon objective research were very critical of government policies aimed at solving this problem. In other words, they were not influenced by the fact that the government had paid for the research.

Essential notes

The findings of Sudhir Venkatesh in *Gang Leader for a Day* were partly shaped by the fact that he liked the people he was supposedly objectively observing.

Essential notes

Functionalist and New Right sociologists tend to stress that modern capitalist societies are characterized by order and consensus. Therefore, they very rarely engage in social dissent or criticism. They are much more likely to uncritically accept and support the way society is currently organized.

This topic continues on the next two pages

For example, functionalist sociologists believe that society is characterized by a consensus on values. Such sociologists tend not to engage in social criticism of the way capitalist societies are organized – instead they support the status quo and thus establishment values. Such sociologists are likely to believe that poverty is the fault of the individual, or working-class culture, or the welfare state, rather than the way capitalism is organized. They are more interested in working-class crime than white-collar or corporate crime. Functionalist sociologists, such as Talcott Parsons, have been accused of being patriarchal, because they believe in distinct gender roles within the family and that only the male should perform the breadwinner role and only the female should perform the nurturing role.

5. Gomm suggests that, by presenting facts as 'truth', sociologists are able to deny responsibility for the way in which their research is used by policy makers. For example, **compensatory education** was introduced into UK schools in the 1960s because sociologists convinced politicians that working-class culture was inferior and required a helping hand in the form of extra resources. However, Gomm points out that this policy distracted from other possible causes of working-class educational underachievement, such as the role of schools and teachers, or the economic or cultural capital enjoyed by the middle classes, or the wealthy's sponsorship of private education. Gomm suggests that the most important aspect of sociological research is what is *not* investigated.

For example, a sociological study of homelessness may investigate the social background of the homeless but may ignore the workings of the property market, which may be responsible for the housing shortage. Such a study will lead only to politically safe conclusions that blame the victims. Gomm suggests that such sociological research is ideological because it helps to maintain inequality.

Critical politicized sociology

Some contemporary sociologists have rejected the concept of value freedom, suggesting that it is undesirable to pretend to be value free. For example, many Marxists feel they should side with the working class and feminists side with women, while many interactionist studies side with the 'deviant'.

Howard Becker argues that sociologists should adopt a compassionate stance and side with the underdogs – criminals, mental patients and other powerless groups – because less is known about these groups and their stories should be told in order to redress the balance of power in society. As a result, interactionists have a strong preference for qualitative methods such as participant observation, which they see as revealing how the 'outsiders' view and interpret the social world.

All these critical perspectives acknowledge that values do and should enter sociological research. Sociologists argue that sociology should not and cannot be morally neutral or indifferent. Instead, it should be **value laden**. Moreover, sociology should be politically prescriptive and suggest ways forward in order to create a better society.

Such ideas do not necessarily mean that the research will be biased and therefore unreliable and invalid. Good sociology still rests on the ability of sociologists to demonstrate the truth of their ideas empirically rather than merely by being committed to certain value positions. Effective sociology still needs to be committed to concepts such as reliability, validity and representativeness.

However, postmodernism rejects the idea that any one sociological account of the social world is superior to another. Any perspective that claims to have the truth, such as Marxism, functionalism or feminism, is just a meta narrative or 'big story'. All knowledge, from any perspective, is based on values and assumptions. Thus, no perspective has any special claim to be true. However postmodernism has been criticized for being logically self-defeating, since it claims to be telling us something true while simultaneously telling us that no one can tell us what is true.

Essential notes

Sociologists are like doctors, who may be motivated by a sense of social justice and emotional commitment to the health of their patients, but this does not mean that they are prevented from conducting an objective investigation into the causes of ill health.

Examiners' notes

Note that in some Theory and Method exam questions the focus may be on whether values can and should be kept out of sociological research. Your response should therefore focus on the debate between those who argue in favour of 'objectivity through neutrality' and those who argue that the whole point of Sociology for sociologists to use their values to change society for the better, for example, Marxists, feminists, Left Realists and Becker.

In order to understand the role of sociology in relation to social policy, it is useful to distinguish between social and sociological problems. Peter Worsley defines a 'social problem' as 'some piece of social behaviour that causes public friction and/or private misery'. For example, poverty, juvenile delinquency and divorce may all be regarded as social problems by members of society, and governments may be called upon to produce policies to tackle the problems.

According to Worsley, a sociological problem is any pattern of social relationships or behaviour. This might be something that society regards as a social problem or behaviour that society does not normally regard as a problem – for example, why people conform or are committed to school or work. In other words, 'normal' behaviour is just as interesting to sociologists as behaviour that people see as a social problem.

The influence of sociology on policy

However, even when sociologists do conduct research into social problems, there is no guarantee that policy makers will use their findings, or that any solutions that sociologists propose will find their way into social policies. There are many factors that affect whether or not sociological research succeeds in influencing government policy including:

- Electoral popularity – research findings might produce a policy that would be unpopular with voters.
- Ideological and policy preferences of governments – if the researcher's value stance is similar to the political ideology of the government, the value stance may stand more chance of influencing its policies. For example, **New Right** sociology has been more successful in persuading recent governments to introduce social policies, especially on crime, than Marxist sociology.
- Interest groups – pressure groups that seek to influence government policies in their own interests; these groups may be powerful enough to persuade the government to ignore sociological research findings.
- Globalization – social policy is increasingly influenced by global interests such as the European Union (EU) and the International Monetary Fund (IMF).
- Critical sociology – sociologists such as Marxists, who are critical of the capitalist state and large corporations, are often ignored by social policy makers.
- Cost – even if the government is sympathetic to the sociologist's findings, it may have other spending priorities and commitments.
- Funding sources – in some cases, sociologists may tone down their findings and policy recommendations because they want to continue to do research in the future and do not want to risk alienating their paymasters.

Perspectives on social policy and sociology

Different sociological perspectives hold different views of the nature of the state and the social policy it produces.

1. Functionalists see the state as serving the interests of society as a whole, to produce and implement rational social policies for the good of all. The sociologist's role is to provide the state with the

objective, scientific information needed to implement social policy effectively. Functionalists usually favour cautious 'piecemeal social engineering', which tackles only one issue at a time.

2. The **social democratic perspective** is more radical and favours a major redistribution of wealth and income from the rich to the poor. Peter Townsend argues that sociologists should be involved in researching social problems such as poverty and should make specific policy recommendations so that social policy can aim to eradicate them.

3. Marxists see the state in capitalist societies as an instrument of the ruling class and its social policies as serving the interests of capitalism rather than the interests of society as a whole. For example, the welfare state exists in order to make it appear as though capitalists care about the poor, the sick and the old. However, the real purpose of the welfare state is to maintain the health and welfare of the working class so that they can be exploited to full effect at work, and to buy off working-class opposition to capitalism. Marxists argue that the only solution to social problems is to overthrow capitalism and create an alternative classless society. The sociologist's job is to reveal to the working class the exploitation and inequality that underpin capitalism so that Marxists can act to do this.

4. Feminists see society as patriarchal, and the state as a patriarchal institution, which perpetuates women's subordination through its social policies. For example, family policies often assume that women should be mostly responsible for nurturing children. However, liberal feminists believe that social policy in the form of anti-discrimination reforms will ultimately bring about gender equality. The radical feminist critique of male violence has led to more positive social policies aimed at tackling domestic violence.

Feminist sociological research has had some impact on social policies in areas that affect women, in part due to the success of the broader feminist movement in gaining greater political influence since the 1970s. For example, social policies such as the 1970 Equal Opportunities Act and the 1975 Equal Pay Act and government attempts to make the education system more girl-friendly were influenced by feminist research that had uncovered gender inequality in both environmentemployment and education.

5. The New Right believe that the state should have minimal involvement in society. They are opposed to using state provision of welfare to deal with social problems. In their view, state intervention in areas such as welfare robs people of their freedom to make their own choices and undermines their sense of responsibility. This, in turn, leads to greater social problems such as crime and delinquency. The New Right also support a strong 'law and order' policy, and research by Right Realist criminologists has been influential in the widespread introduction of zero tolerance crime policies.

Essential notes

Marxists claim that both the functionalist and social democratic approaches fail to deal with the real cause of inequality, which is the way capitalism is organized.

Essential notes

Critics argue that Marxist views on social policy and the role of sociologists are impractical and unrealistic.

Essential notes

New Right thinking has been very influential on Labour and Conservative governments with regard to family and crime policies. For example, both situational and environmental crime policies which are products of New Right thinking, have been adopted by recent governments.

Essential notes

There are essentially three perspectives in the debate about the relationship between sociology and social policy.

1. Those who believe that sociologists should bot concern themselves with the way social-policymakers use their research.

2. The New Right view which believes that the state and social policy interferes too much in people's lives.

3. Marxists, feminists, social democrats and left realists who believe that the State should use social policy to change society for the better.

General tips for A-level Sociology Paper 3 Crime and Deviance with Theory and Methods

Paper 3 Crime and Deviance with Theory and Methods is compulsory and consists of six compulsory questions, to be completed in two hours. The maximum mark for this paper is 80 (50 marks for Crime and Deviance, 30 marks for Theory and Methods). This is under 1.5 minutes per mark, once you have taken off time for reading. Remember to allocate your time according to the number of marks in each question. All exam questions carrying 10 marks or more should be written in continuous prose and you will be assessed on your use of good English, organization and appropriate sociological terminology.

Approximately 45% of the overall marks for Paper 3 are for AO1 (knowledge and understanding of theories, concepts, evidence and research). However, AO2 (application) and AO3 (analysis and evaluation) are very important, particularly for the long answer, essay and application questions. At A level, you are expected to show that you can interpret questions well and then apply relevant material to answer the question. You should also show good analysis and evaluation skills – you need to unpack and discuss issues, not just describe theories and research. You will also show these skills by having a clear focus on the question set and answering it directly, rather than writing in general about the topic area. You may refer back to the question and this often helps you to stay on track. You will be given three Items to help you with some of the questions. Once you are familiar with the questions, read the items carefully to identify points or issues you can use. Bear in mind that the Items only provide you with a starting point. These are not comprehension questions and the Item material needs to be further analysed and evaluated. Your response will also need to apply the material and show how it is relevant to the question.

Crime and deviance

- **Question 01** is a short-answer question on Crime and Deviance, worth 4 marks. You will be asked **to outline two ways/ patterns/ trends/reasons:** for example, two reasons why statistics for ethnic offending are higher, or two ways in which the media affects people's perceptions of the crime rate. The likelihood is that you will need to write an identifier (the reason) and a qualifier (the explanation) to achieve the full 4 marks. You may want to write two separate paragraphs, or even use the phrase 'one way could be'. Be mindful of time: the question is worth **4 marks** and you should avoid spending too long on it; 4 or 5 minutes maximum.

- **Question 02** is worth **6 marks**. It will ask you for **three reasons** for a social happening. Again, you must fully explain the reason to get the full 6 marks. One mark is awarded for the reason (identifier), and 1 mark is awarded for the development or explanation of the identifier. You might be asked for three reasons why women are more likely to be victims of crime:
  - One identifier could be they are seen as vulnerable (1 mark).
  - Women are stereotyped as being weak and therefore they are targeted (+1).
  - Women as victims of rape (1 mark).
  - Studies show that women who are out late at night or dress in a promiscuous way are more likely to be suitable rape victims (+1).
  - Domestic violence (1 mark).

- Studies show that women are more likely to be victims of domestic assaults and one incident occurs every 60 seconds in the UK (+1). Be very clear that you have provided three answers: you can use the identifiers 1, 2 and 3 if it helps, or three separate sentences. You could even put them on different lines. You can give more than three reasons, as the examiner will mark all of your reasons and credit the best ones.

- **Question 03** is a long-answer application question with an accompanying item. It is worth **10 marks**. It will you ask **to apply** the material the Item and analyse two things. It is important in this response to find two points from the item and apply them to the question. Show how they are relevant to the answer. To gain higher marks, it is important that you analyse and evaluate the two points you have identified from the Item. You can do this by using further sociological knowledge, evidence and concepts, explaining whether they support the points or not and using developed reasoning. The Item will guide you, helping to shape your ideas, but should not just be recycled. The discussion could focus on issues such as why they are significant and how significant they are. Perhaps what impact they have had on sociology or society. To get into the top mark band (8–10), you will need good knowledge and understanding, to apply it clearly and to include analysis and evaluation. It may be worthwhile including a one- or two-sentence conclusion linking your two points and evaluating how important each of them is. Marks are awarded for the overall quality of both examples together, rather than 5 marks per example. As this answer is worth 10 marks, it must be written in continuous prose.

- **Question 04** is a **30-mark essay question** with an accompanying item. It will ask you **to apply** material from Item B and your knowledge **to evaluate** something. In this response you should build upon the item and develop a wider range of reasons and relevant material, adding breadth and depth to your answer. In this response you are showing that you have detailed, accurate and developed knowledge and are able to draw upon concepts and research to develop your answers. For higher marks you must also make sure you apply your answer fully and show how each of the arguments and points that you have developed are relevant to the question. Finally, the question will ask you to evaluate. A higher-level answer will do this throughout the response and regularly weigh up the points developed, the quality of the evidence used and consider whether this strengthens or weakens the arguments considered.

    To answer this question, like other longer questions, this is marked using mark bands, and your aim should be to get as high up as you can in the highest mark bands you can get into. The top mark band gains you 25 to 30 marks, and for this you will be expected to have detailed knowledge and a strong understanding with the use of plenty of concepts; you will have to apply your material well to the question, and have clear and explicit evaluation of the strengths and weaknesses of different arguments leading to a conclusion. As a minimum you will need to explain the view in the question, look at theories and/or evidence and/or arguments to support this view, do the same with views, theories, arguments and evidence which do not support the statement, and reach a conclusion about the strengths of the arguments of the two sides. To make sure that the material you use to answer the question meets the demands of the question, you may find it useful to refer back to the question at several stages, as this will help you to stay on track and on topic.

Theory and methods

- **Question 05** is a **10-mark question**. It will ask you **to outline** and **explain** two things. It has a similar format to the 'Outline and explain' questions on AS Papers 1 and 2. This question needs you to give a developed outline of two key factors, such as reasons, causes, advantages, disadvantages and so on. In addition, you must also give developed reasoning that demonstrates an extended understanding and explanation of the factors identified.

  To answer this question you must clearly identify your two points. Each point must be opened up and fully developed. You might decide to choose practical strengths or weaknesses, such as time and ease. You might choose theoretical strengths or weakness, such as large sample sizes, or the ability to gain valid results. You might choose ethical strengths and weaknesses, such as little deception or participant involvement. This question may want to know why sociologists conduct research in a certain way or why they do something. It is worth referring to a glossary on key terms within research methods to make sure you can explain them all. As this answer is worth 10 marks, it must be written in continuous prose.

- **Question 06** is a **20-mark essay question** with an accompanying item. It will ask, 'Applying material from Item C and your knowledge, evaluate...'. A successful response for this question needs to show accurate and detailed knowledge of sociological theory and methods. Marks are also given for application, analysis and evaluation. Similar to Question 04, for higher marks you will need to make sure that the response remains focused and applied throughout and that it does not lapse into describing general sociological theory. To evaluate and analyse contrasting theories and methods, you may want to compare them with alternative theories and methods or weigh up their advantages and disadvantages. This may need to be applied to the context of the question or item. This question is marked in bands, and to gain access to the higher band, which is the 17–20 mark band, you will need a range of points, good analysis and evaluation. When writing essays, you should look back regularly to the question. Make sure you have obeyed all the instructions and covered all the issues included in the question. Some essays have two or more parts. You will not gain top marks if you do not address each part. It's also very important to focus on the question set. Do not be tempted to write an essay about all you know on a topic in a question, or to spend time writing at a tangent to the question – use your material to focus on the issues.

Crime and deviance (sample A-level exam Paper 3)

Questions

01 Outline **two** strategies for reducing crime. **[4 marks]**

02 Outline **three** reasons why rates of offending amongst ethnic groups are higher. **[6 marks]**

03 Read **Item A** below and answer the question that follows.

> ## Item A
>
> Postmodernists support the idea that society has undergone some radical changes. One of the biggest changes and developments is globalization and the rise of technology. Globalization has allowed the world to become a more interconnected place as people from one country can get in touch with others far away with ease. The rise in technology means that it has become part of everyday life for many individuals. Not only can people keep in touch by using the internet but they can also perform a range of tasks online.

Applying material from **Item A**, analyse two ways in which the type of crime in society is changing. **[10 marks]**

04 Read **Item B** below and answer the question that follows.

> ## Item B
>
> In many cities across the UK young groups of people get together. Many of these groups are known as gangs and there is a link between crime and gangs. Gangs are mainly made up of young males. Some may join because they are bored, or because they gain a sense of satisfaction from the group. It can be problematic for society if groups of people are acting in a criminal and deviant way.

Applying material from **Item B** and your knowledge, evaluate the usefulness of the subcultural approaches in understanding crime and deviance. **[30 marks]**

05 Outline and explain **two** advantages of using unstructured interviews in sociological research. **[10 marks]**

06 Read **Item C** below and answer the question that follows.

> ## Item C
>
> Feminists see a societal conflict between men and women. Men are able to control women and are given more power in every aspect of social life. This creates inequalities for women in all spheres of life.
>
> Different feminists have different areas of concerns and different approaches for making society equal for men and women.

Applying material from **Item C** and your knowledge, evaluate the usefulness of feminist approaches in understanding society. **[20 marks]**

Grade C answers

01 *Outline **two** strategies for reducing crime.* **[4 marks]**

One strategy for reducing crime is in the environment. This is where everybody can help. A second strategy for reducing crime is situational. **[Mark: 2/4]**

This candidate has identified two appropriate strategies for crime prevention but has failed to achieve the award for the development of them – for example, the answer scored 1 for identifying environmental prevention but the explanation is not enough for the second mark. A mark is also awarded for another partial response, as situational crime prevention scores 1 mark but is not developed for the second.

The first reason the answer given scores the full two marks: the candidate has identified poverty as a reason and developed it enough to gain the second mark by explaining it's to help with living. The second two reasons score partially, as both identify a reason but then fail to develop the explanation.

02 *Outline **three** reasons why rates of offending amongst ethnic groups are higher.* **[6 marks]**

One reason rates of offending are higher for ethnic minorities is poverty, as they may have to commit crime to help them live. Another reason is material deprivation. Another reason is because of subcultures they join. **[Mark: 4/6]**

03 *Applying material from **Item A**, analyse two ways in which the type of crime in society is changing.* **[10 marks]**

Item A states that the type of crime in society is changing because of technology. Technology is now a part of nearly everybody's lives on a daily basis. People spend lots of time on the internet, and this means there is more opportunity to commit crime. Lots of different types of crime can be committed on the internet. This is known as cyber-crime. One type of cybercrime is fraud, this can be stealing somebody's identity, and this can be done by watching their activity when they are online. Another is hacking, or getting people's information without them knowing. The item also discusses globalization. This means there are new types of crime because people from all over the world can commit crime together. **[Mark: 5/10]**

This answer is placed in the second band, which is 4–7. The candidate does provide two ways in which crime is changing. However, the second remains underdeveloped. The first way in which crime has changed does display some development. The candidate has made use of the item but has also shown expansion, as they have been able to develop the ways in which increased technology has led to crime. They use a sociological concept by discussing cybercrime. The candidate is also able to describe some types of cybercrime but fails to elaborate any further. Because the second way in which crime has changed is left undeveloped, this candidate scores no higher than 5.

---

04 *Applying material from **Item B** and your knowledge, evaluate the usefulness of the subcultural approaches in understanding crime and deviance.* [**30 marks**]

A subculture is a group of people in society. The item states these are usually young people. This means that there could be lots of groups committing crime not just individuals. The theory which tries to explain this is subcultural theory.

> The student makes a basic attempt to define a subculture and makes use of the item.

Two subcultural theorists are Cloward and Ohlin. They came up with the illegitimate opportunity structure. This means that some people can be successful in illegal ways.

> The student has identified the target theory.

They said that there were three possible subcultures a person could join: criminal, conflict and retreatist. People who join a criminal subculture can join young and work their way up to the top. Conflict is more about gang warfare. Those who join retreatist subcultures do not have many opportunities so they retreat into a world of drugs and alcohol. This theory can be criticized though, as there is no proof that just three subcultures exist.

> The knowledge in this paragraph is accurate. However, it lacks application, the candidate does not manage to apply supporting examples. The candidate also makes an evaluative statement but it is basic and simplistic, and could be developed.

Another sociologist who looked at subcultures is Cohen. Cohen linked subcultural membership to the education system. Boys do not do as well as girls in the education system and they get fewer qualifications. This means that they struggle to get good jobs when they leave school so they have status frustration. This is seen in Willis's study of working class boys in school. They join anti school subcultures. They can gain status from the subcultures which they will not get from work. Feminists don't like this as there is no discussion of status frustration for girls.

> The candidate has applied a relevant study from education but fails to really develop it.

A final subcultural idea comes from Miller who said that young groups of boys have focal concerns. These are smartness, trouble, excitement and fate. Trouble is the idea that young groups of boys may not go out looking for trouble but they just so happen to find it. On a night out they may have had lots to drink so they end up in a fight. They may not have really meant to do so but it just happened. Again this can be criticized because it does not discuss females: girls are also going out at night and getting into fights.

> Here the candidate makes another evaluative statement, which is more developed than the previous one, as a sociological theory s used.

> Again, a suitable example is applied to the answer, which displays a deeper level of knowledge.

> This is a reasonable evaluative statement and draws a comparison with females.

> Reasonable knowledge is displayed here; most of the focal concerns are named.

Student makes use of the item for a second time.

Then there is Matza. He doesn't think that subcultures exist which goes against the item. Matza argues that young people do not join subcultures but instead they give in to subterranean values. This means that they make excuses for their behaviour. He called this 'techniques of neutralisation' including denial of responsibility. This means that they don't think it is their fault.

Although this is good knowledge, there is limited development.

Subcultural theory is good because there are gangs in the UK, but it doesn't explain all crime in the UK. **[Mark: 18/30]**

Although basic, a conclusion is offered. This answer displays largely accurate knowledge which does have some range. However, it lacks depth, which is why it is placed in the 13–18 band. There are two/ three isolated statements of evaluation, which remain underdeveloped.

05 *Outline and explain **two** advantages of using unstructured interviews in sociological research.* **[10 marks]**

One advantage of unstructured interviews is that they are flexible. They are more like conversations and can go in any direction. This is good when you are studying sensitive topics because the person being interviewed has more control. You can go off topic and maybe uncover things you didn't think you would because they are not structured and are flexible. Another advantage of unstructured interviews is ethics. They are good for ethics. It will not be the first time the interviewer has met the participant; they will have already met. This means that the interviewee will feel comfortable with the interviewer and they will be relaxed. They won't be in any harm as it is ethical. **[Mark: 6/10]**

This answer displays two clear concise advantages of unstructured interviews and it is placed in the 4–7 band. The first is more developed and the candidate clearly knows the format the research method takes and why this is an advantage. The second shows knowledge but lacks some development. There is little analysis, which is why this answer scores 6.

This is a basic introduction, but it does make use of the item and shows some understanding of patriarchy.

06 *Applying material from **Item C** and your knowledge, evaluate the usefulness of feminist approaches in understanding society.* **[20 marks]**

Item C states that there is inequality between men and women. This is known as patriarchy, the idea feminists present that society benefits men more than it does women.

The candidate shows a reasonable amount of knowledge of feminism, which is drawn from the item. They have failed to add difference feminism to their knowledge.

There are different types of feminism: liberal, Marxist and radical. Each type has things that they are campaigning to change, as stated in the item. All of them want to make things better for women.

Liberal feminism is the most common type. Liberal feminists want to make things better for women by changing laws and policy. For example both the equal pay act and the sex discrimination act are polices which have been

This is good knowledge.

implemented to make things fair for women. However it could be argued that both these acts are weak and do not really offer women enough support. Ann Oakley is a liberal feminist and she has helped us to understand how the family is not an equal place for women. Oakley conducted research on the amount of housework that women do and she discovered that over 80% of women take sole responsibility for housework and looking after children whereas for men it's less. This shows that things in the family are not equal for men and women. Radical feminists have also helped us understand what family life is like for women as they think that the family is oppressive and women are the victims of domestic violence. A study by Dobash and Dobash found that women are abused in the home and that two women a week will die in the UK as a result of domestic violence. They found that women do not tend to report this enough and that roughly 1 in 4 women will be a victim. This is shocking. It is also worth noting that the rates of violence on men in the family is rising and it's not just women anymore.

This is not like functionalism. Functionalists do not think that the family is unequal; they think that is equal. Parsons believes that men and women have roles that they must play within the family. Women are suited to the housework and looking after the children. This is known as the expressive role. Men they go out to work and bring home the money for the family. This is known as the instrumental role.

Radical feminists don't like men. They think that women should be lesbians. It is the most extreme form of feminism. They think that men treat women like sex objects and they just dominate them. They think women need to get back power and lead lives that are separate to men. This wouldn't work though.

I think that one of the best ways that feminism has helped us to understand the inequalities that women face is within the workplace. Women earn less than men and they still cannot get into the top positions. Most people who work in finance are men and most senior judges and barristers are men. Women can see the top but they can't get there. Ann Oakley called this the glass ceiling. Things are changing though in the UK, as some women can get to the top and hold some senior positions. For example we now have our second female Prime Minister which is a good thing for women. Women can also use the equal pay act if they do not feel that they are being paid fairly. This shows that things are getting better.

Feminists have helped us to understand how things in society are unequal in a number of different ways. **[Mark: 15/20]**

Good link to policy.

Here is a simple evaluation, the candidate misses an opportunity to develop this further and could give an example.

This knowledge is accurate but lacks depth. A chance to analyse and evaluate has also been missed.

This statement shows some sophistication, the candidate is aware of current UK issues and draw a comparison with men.

This paragraph is juxtaposition. The candidate clearly has some knowledge on functionalism, but the way this is used is not focused on the target aspect theory of the question. It could have been used to evaluate but it is not.

Incomplete knowledge.

Incomplete knowledge – this could have been developed to state how and why.

Very simple evaluation.

Inaccurate knowledge applied to concept. Here the candidate shows they understand the concept of the glass ceiling but Ann Oakley did not coin the term.

This is a good link to the contemporary UK.

Some deeper analysis and evaluation here.

This is a basic conclusion. This answer is placed in the 14-16 band because its lacks depth and range. The knowledge is mostly accurate but remains underdeveloped in places. There is also a lack of analysis and evaluation, which is why it is placed in this band.

Grade A answers

01 *Outline **two** strategies for reducing crime.* [**4 marks**]

One strategy for crime prevention is situational crime prevention which is a right Realist idea. This mainly looks at ways to reduce crime: for example, installing more CCTV would reduce crime. A second strategy of crime prevention is community crime prevention where local residents can be active in trying to reduce crime, for example they could create a local neighbourhood watch group. [**Mark: 4/4**]

This answer achieved full marks because it shows excellent and accurate knowledge. The candidate clearly identifies two crime prevention strategies, and therefore achieves both marks available for identification. Both of the crime prevention strategies are then developed with examples, clearly showing the candidate understands what they are. This achieves the second 2 marks.

02 *Outline **three** reasons why rates of offending amongst ethnic groups are higher.* [**6 marks**]

The first reason why rates of offending are higher among ethnic minorities is that they are more likely to join deviant subcultures, perhaps because they failed at school and can gain status from a subcultural group. The second reason is that they may be suffering from material deprivation, which means they can see other people around them with more material goods than themselves and they want these things, so they turn to crime. A final reason is that they are marginalized in society. [**Mark: 5/6**]

This answer clearly identifies three distinct reasons for higher rates of offending for ethnic minority members of the population. It therefore scores 3 marks for the identification. The first reasons are developed and score a further 2 marks. However, the final reason is not, so it only scores 1 out of a possible 2 for the identifier of marginalization.

03 *Applying material from **Item A**, analyse two ways in which the type of crime in society is changing.* [**10 marks**]

Globalization means the world is becoming smaller and is interconnected (Item A). This means that people in one country can contact those in another country with great ease. It also means that we can travel the world with more ease and national boarders are disintegrating, Postmodernists (Item A) believe this means that there has been a growth in new organized crime. It is simple: if criminals all over the world can contact each other they will. For example there has been a rise in the illegal sale of ivory. This ivory comes from Africa yet it is sold to China and Malaysia which would not be possible if it were not organized. Another example which is more serious is human trafficking. This is really serious as much of time it is women and children who are sold and shipped all over the world. It is new concern of feminists. A second new type of crime that has emerged as a result of globalisation is cybercrime. We now use computers more so than ever before and we are digital natives. Computers are part of our everyday lives and we can do many things on them (Item A) like online banking, which allows criminals the opportunity to steal our details. They can hack into our accounts or log our movements in order to gain access to our bank accounts and personal details. They could even try and get a loan or purchase products with our credit cards. It is called identity theft. People also use emails to communicate more freely than ever before and people are sometimes sent so called phishing emails which try to extort money out of people fraudulently. The internet is a place which can help us with our day to day activities but also it creates crime. This wasn't around 50 years ago because we didn't use the internet so it is all new. **[Mark: 10/10]**

> This candidate achieves full marks for this answer because it is conceptually detailed and accurate. The candidate provides two distinct and new types of crime, which are frequently relayed back to the Item. Examples are given for both new types of crime, which are detailed and developed. There is a good level of analysis.

---

04 *Applying material from **Item B** and your knowledge, evaluate the usefulness of the subcultural approaches in understanding crime and deviance.* **[30 marks]**

Item C suggests that groups of gangs are problematic for many major cities in the UK. The problem is that if a group of people choose to act in a criminal and deviant way the result could be far worse than a person acting alone. The Chicago school of sociology was one of the first to develop subcultural theory as it was a growing problem in Chicago at the time.

> This is a strong introduction; not only does it use the item, but it displays knowledge of the wider origins of subcultural theory.

Subcultural theory draws on the work of Merton, who although he did not specifically discuss subcultures, analysed the idea of strain. Strain occurs when people cannot achieve the American Dream (material wealth and goals) via legitimate means. Merton discussed five responses to strain some of which were criminal and deviant. Cloward and Ohlin believe Merton has failed to develop the idea of achieving things illegitimately and therefore that's what their study focused on. Cloward and Ohlin believed that there were two opportunity structures in this world, the legal opportunity structure and the illegitimate opportunity structure. The legitimate opportunity structure causes no problems and links to Merton's idea of conformity. Most people will stick to law and abide by the rules even if they aren't succeeding as they still believe this is the only way. The illegitimate opportunity structure is different and can provide a way to get the means in an illegal way. Cloward and Ohlin suggested that if an individual went down the illegitimate route then there were three possible subcultures they could join. The first is a criminal subculture. This is where there is a thriving criminal underworld in an area and people are able to join at a young age. They can learn and rise up through the ranks potentially having a criminal career. This is supported in Bourgios study of El arrio. Bourgios studied Latin Americans who have come to live in New York full of the ideas that America would provide

This whole paragraph displays knowledge and understanding which will be placed in the top band, as it is wide-ranging and detailed. The candidate uses Merton but also applies the knowledge of Cloward and Ohlin. This is the first point which is made of the target aspect of the theory. The point clearly shows excellent knowledge and the application is also excellent, using Bourgios as a supporting study. The candidate then makes an excellent evaluative statement by giving a strength and weaknesses. They also use sociological theory in an appropriate way.

The correct Cohen theory identified.

Another sophisticated point. Good knowledge is shown and applied with the use of a supporting study and comprehensive evaluation, which displays both strengths and weaknesses. This is what to expect from a top band answer.

This is the third point on the target aspect of the theory, showing a wide range of knowledge. This paragraph displays excellent knowledge. All six focal concerns are listed. The candidate does not open up all of them but be mindful of the time constraints of the question. Miller is then evaluated with the use of Katz.

them a better life. When they got there they realized that they were unequal to Americans and life was hard. In turn they then turned to crime to succeed. They had makeshift roadside garages and mainly sold crack cocaine to make money. This is a good study because it shows that groups can make a success of things illegally. It was also a longitudinal study and therefore shows great validity. The next subculture that Cloward Ohlin discussed was the conflict subculture. This is where there is no thriving criminal underworld to join but an individual can join a conflict gang. Conflict gangs fight rivals for territory and gain status that way. At first you could argue this is not relevant as the study was from Chicago but as the Item states gangs are a problem in UK cities and many of them are violent conflict gangs. The third subculture an individual could join is retreatist. This is where one of the other two subcultures are not available and a person retreats into a world of drugs and alcohol. The problem with this study is it assumes that there are three neat distinctions for subcultures, however they are more complex. Marxists are also critical of this as Cloward and Ohlin fail to explore power relationships or inequalities, some people join subcultures because of the structure of society.

Albert Cohen also looked at subcultural theory. He did disagree with Merton though, as he was interested in why much of the crime and delinquent behaviour had no material gain. Cohen suggested that whilst at schools lower class males had middle class values of which they aspired to. It soon transpired that they would be unable to achieve these in the normal way through good education. They suffered from something he called status frustration. This is a sense of injustice at the position they have been put in. To combat this they join subcultures, as these groups of boys can give them the status that they cannot get through education and a good job. This has been supported by Paul Willis's study 'Learning to Labour' where the young boys in his study join anti school subcultures in order to gain respect from their peers. Further support would also come from education statistics. Year on year, girls outperform boys in the education system so it could be argued that Cohen is correct and boys do get status frustration. However feminists have criticized this study as there is no discussion of females. Jackson did a study on ladette culture and discovered that girls too were playing up at school forming anti school subcultures in order to gain respect from their peers.

Walter Miller studied subcultural theory. However rather than explaining what drove young men to join subcultures he set out to explain the criminal and deviant behaviour in them, Miller stated that young lower class subcultures had focal concerns. These focal concerns linked them with crime, deviancy and delinquency. The focal concerns are trouble, fate, autonomy, smartness, excitement and smartness. For example if we take excitement, young men would not be drawn to these groups if it were not exciting. They provide a sense of fun in a somewhat a boring lifestyle. The idea that they do not go looking for trouble but it seems to find them can be displayed in the lifestyles they adopt. So by going into the night time economy they are faced with alcohol and violence which means they end up in trouble. Katz is dismissive of this idea though. Katz has suggested that it is not only groups of males that commit crime because it is exciting but most young people because they are seduced by crime it is thrilling. It's not about subcultures; it is about seeking thrills.

Matza disagrees wholly with subcultural theory and argues that subcultures do not exist. Matza does not think that deviants hold different norms and values to the rest of society (subcultures). Instead Matza argues that everybody has two sets of values: conventional and subterranean. Subterranean are deviant ones which according to Matza everybody has. It just depends if you act on them. Young people are not predisposed to joining subcultures; they act on their deviant values because they use what Matza named techniques of neutralisation to justify their behaviour. Therefore Matza concludes the use of subculture is exaggerated, and subcultures do not exist.

It is clear to see that subcultural theory is helpful. As item C states there is a problem in the UK with gangs and if we can gain an insight into the problem it could be beneficial to help prevent them. For example if Cohen's status frustration proves to be correct more could be done to help boys in school. However there is a distinct lack of discussion of female deviancy. Feminists would argue the whole theory is malestream. Girls also join subcultures. **[Mark: 28/30]**

> Another good paragraph displaying knowledge. This point is in a reflective tone, also displaying evaluative skills. Opportunity missed to list/delve into the techniques of neutralizsation.

> This fully supported critical conclusion links in the item. It displays sound conceptually detailed knowledge, which is why it is placed in the top band. Appropriate material is applied and comprehensive evaluations are made using another sociological theory.

---

05 *Outline and explain **two** advantages of using unstructured interviews in sociological research.* **[10 marks]**

An unstructured interview does not have any questions and is not planned. Instead it takes the form of a guided conversation. One advantage of using unstructured interview is the rich detailed qualitative data you can gather. Interpretivists prefer this type of data collection because it is high in validity. This means it is true to life. Data is collected in the form of words and thoughts and feelings. No other method of data collection can achieve this. An unstructured interview is conversational and therefore there is free flowing conversation which is true to life. All of the material can be recorded, transcribed and used later. Because it so informal the participant is likely to tell the truth so it is high in validity. Positivists would argue that reliability is low. Positivists would also criticize the lack of numbers produced and the replicability of the method.

Another strength of using unstructured interviews is that they are good to use when wanting to get to sensitive issues. As previously stated they are much less formal than other research methods. Participants are relaxed and they will open up about things which they wouldn't usually about sensitive topics. Feminists favour this method. For example Ann Oakley used unstructured interviews to gather data on pregnancy and childbirth. This is a sensitive topic and not everybody would want to discuss it. It is personal but given this method is more like a conversation you are able to discuss sensitive things.

Above all unstructured interviews are high in validity and give rich in depth data. **[Mark: 10/10]**

> This candidate has correctly identified two clear advantages. Both are detailed and display in-depth knowledge. The candidate is also able to apply the relevant theory by using both interpretivism and feminism. There is appropriate analysis through the comparison with positivism and that's why this achieves full marks.

06 *Applying material from **Item C** and your knowledge, evaluate the usefulness of feminist approaches in understanding society.* [**20 marks**]

This is a strong introduction. The candidate makes good use of the item and shows understanding of patriarchy. The candidate has also indentifed four different types of feminism and different areas of social life where women would face inequality.

Item C states that the lives of men and women are unequal. This inequality between men and women is known as patriarchy. Feminists use the word patriarchy to describe how society benefits men and places women in subordinate positions. Feminism is a conflict theory and feminists believe that conflict exists in all areas of society as suggested by item C. Some of main areas where women face such inequality are the home, the workplace, education and within the field of crime. The item also suggests that there are different types of feminists known as Liberal, Marxist, Radical and difference. All of the different feminist theories help us to understand how things work in a male dominated society.

Liberal feminism is the most common type of feminism and liberal feminists not only want to get to the root of patriarchy but to change things for women through legal reform. Ann Oakley is a liberal feminist and she argues that the patriarchal nature of society begins in the home during gender role socialisation. Oakley believed that parents gender role socialize their children in four ways. The first is manipulation; this where they manipulate the child's behaviour. For example if a little boy fell they would tell him to get up and not to cry, because big boys don't cry. The second is canalisation. This is where the children's interests are channelled by the parents with regards to what is seen appropriate for each gender. For example buying dolls for girls and toy soldiers for boys. The third is through verbal appellations this is the use of gendered terms for boys and girls such as 'little princess'. The fourth and final way is through different activities, such as girls helping their mums with baking and boys helping their dads with the DIY. This can clearly been seen in households up and down the UK and also matches up with the functionalist Parsons' idea about the instrumental and expressive roles. Ann Oakley is concerned that if this does not change then children will continue to be gender role socialized in the same way and things will never change. This is a good way to look at social inequality because it explains where patriarchy begins. It is worth noting though that not all families gender socialize their children in this way and many parents challenge gender roles. Also postmodernists note there has been a rise in same-sex couples who would also challenge these assumptions.

This is a sophisticated paragraph which shows in-depth knowledge and understanding. There is clear use of key sociological concepts and knowledge is explicitly applied to the question. There is good level of analysis and evaluation at the end, with a link to the Families and Households topic.

Marxist feminists share both the same concerns as Marxists but also a feminist viewpoint. So if males from the proletariat are exploited then so too will the women be. In fact it could be argued that women are further exploited because of the nature of capitalism and because of the role they are given. Margaret Benston who is a Marxist feminist claimed that women are just the 'reserve army of labour'. They keep the men fit and healthy and look after the home and children so the men can keep going back to work. That is what is best for capitalism to work. However when the women are needed in the workforce they can step in. This happened in WW2 where many women played important roles in the workforce but when the men came back they went back into their traditional roles. The role that women are given in raising the children and doing all of the housework is also exploitative as it is free and unpaid. If the government had to pay women for this it would cost money. The role is also devalued as it's seen as only housework. This means that women are not taken as seriously in the workplace. This explanation that feminists put forward can be used to help us understand gender inequality within the workplace. It's estimated that on average women earn 25% less than men even of the same job. Women still fail to reach the top positions. Walby looked at how women were also viewed as unsuitable bosses. It appears that despite the equal pay act and gender discrimination act women still face the glass ceiling in the workplace: they can see the top but they cannot get there.

Radical feminists have helped us to understand some of the most harrowing issues for women. Radical feminism is the most extreme type of feminism because it looks at control and patriarchy through sexual control and political dominance. For example radical feminist have highlighted some of the issues that happen in family life which put women in a vulnerable position. Domestic violence and sexual assault within the family is a dark side of family life which unfortunately happens to around 1 in 4 women. Domestic violence was once a taboo issue for society and sociology. The functionalist perspective saw men and women having roles such as expressive and instrumental and the family was seen as a private domain. Domestic disputes within the family were also seen as a private matter and until the 1980s the police were reluctant to attend. However feminists helped social thinking towards this change. Finally in 1991 the rape amendment act came in force which made marital rape illegal. This is concerning, considering how late this act came, and domestic issues are still a serious issue for many families. Dobash and Dobash studied domestic violence in the family and discovered some shocking facts. One incident of domestic violence occurs every 60 seconds in the UK. Two women a week will lose their lives to domestic violence and that violence is more likely to take place in the evening. It is a positive thing that feminists have made sure that these issues are brought to society's attention. For example the police now take this more seriously. They now have cameras on their helmets and officers are specifically training for domestics. This is positive thing. However, it is worth noting that the number of male victims of domestic violence is on the rise which feminist explanations do not take into account. Further support for the radical feminist view point of domestic violence came from Leach who suggested that the nuclear family was like a simmering pot waiting to boil over and that is was prone to violence.

The final type of feminism is known as difference feminism. Item C suggests that different feminist theories have different concerns. Difference feminists are keen to point out that the lives of white western women have improved drastically however the lives of women around the world still have some way to go. Sawaadi is a difference feminist who herself was subjected to female genital mutilation. Barbaric acts still happen to women all over the world and difference feminists explore such issues. For example forced marriage still occurs in countries like Iran and Pakistan and some girls are being forced to marry very young. Yousef Malala also campaigned for the education of young girls being a standard in some Muslim countries. So it is clear to see that gender inequality is still bad in some parts of the world.

Another good paragraph, with a second aspect of feminism. Good knowledge and understanding is applied. The evaluation is weaker than the first point but it is still evident.

This paragraph shows good knowledge of radical feminism but lacks some depth with the main underpinning of the target aspect of the theory. Material from the sociology of the family is in-depth and accurate and sensitively applied to the question. A good example is used, which is linked to social policy. This is also evaluated, with a strength and weakness, and a link is made to the question.

This displays excellent knowledge of difference feminism, good contemporary examples are applied. There is only basic evaluation here.

The candidate makes a good link back to the question and is able to reach a critical conclusion. This answer is placed in the top mark bracket and scores 19. This is because it is sound and conceptually detailed. Knowledge is accurately applied to the question and the evaluation is of a high standard.

Some sociological theories only suggest policy ideas or theorize about certain topics, whereas feminism does actually make social change through new social policy and changes in legislation. So the feminist perspective does offer us a great deal when understanding society and gender inequality. However with the main concern of feminists being patriarchy other types of social inequality are not explored by the feminist perspective. **[Mark: 19/20]**

More sample questions

01 Outline two ways in which deviancy could be functional for society. **[4 marks]**

02 Outline three reasons why some people are more likely to be victims of crime. **[6 marks]**

03 Read **Item A** below and answer the question that follows.

Item A

The media is a source of information for the whole of society and comes in many different forms. The media is often accused of sending a range of messages to the general public. A key concern of sociologists is that some people choose to accept the messages that they are sent in media. This means that people are forming biased opinions about different social groups, and these may not be based on facts.

Applying material from **Item A**, analyse two reasons why some groups are labelled by the media. **[10 marks]**

04 Read **Item B** below and answer the question that follows.

Item B

Marxists highlight many issues with regards to crime and deviance in society. They argue that levels of crime are not always representative of the true picture of crime. They argue that there is a dark figure of crime, as some crimes are underrepresented and underpunished. Marxists argue that crime and deviancy could be a way to control the masses.

Applying material from **Item B** and your knowledge, evaluate the usefulness of Marxist approaches in understanding crime and deviance. **[30 marks]**

05 Outline and explain **two** advantages of using secondary data in sociological research. [**10 marks**]

06 Read **Item C** below and answer the question that follows.

Item C

Sociological research has always aimed to provide knowledge on social problems with a view to also provide potential solutions. Sociologists gather research on all aspects of social life. Without the research that sociologists conduct, we would not have collected data or provided answers for some serious issues in society such as inequalities within the education system or the family.

Applying material from **Item C** and your knowledge, evaluate the contribution of sociology on social policy. [**20 marks**]

Question 6 Education and Methods Paper 1 (Theory focus)

Q6 Outline and explain two ways in which society is still patriarchal. [**10 marks**]

Grade C answer

One way in which society is still patriarchal is in the family. Studies show that women are still doing the majority of the housework. Ann Oakley studied this and she said that men just help out. Functionalists state that women are more suited to this role of a home maker and they call it the expressive role. Women are naturally caring and nurturing, therefore they will have to stay at home and raise the children because it meets the needs of society.

Another way in society is patriarchal is in the education system. Even though girls have made much progress in school, things are still gendered. Girls are not given enough encouragement to study more masculine subjects, especially at A-level, such as the sciences. Not many girls take physics and chemistry at A-level which means not many go onto university to study these subjects. This means girls are limited into pursuing certain careers. It could be because there are a lack of female role models in these subjects. [**Mark: 6/10**]

This candidate has suggested two clear and distinct areas of social life which are patriarchal. Knowledge in this response is good, but it lacks depth. There is some very limited analysis, which is why it scores in the 4–7 band.

Grade A answer

Patriarchy is the concept feminists use to describe the conflict between men and women in society. Feminists argue that all areas of society are patriarchal and benefit men more than women.

One important area where patriarchy can still be seen is within the workplace. More women have entered the workforce in the last 30 years, yet they do not occupy the top positions and there is still a gender pay gap. Feminists argue that there is a glass ceiling in place for women in the workplace, where they can see the top but they cannot reach it. This can been supported by Hakims idea of vertical segregation. Hakim suggests that women occupy lower levels of pay and status in the jobs sector. Barron and Norris supported this idea with the dual labour market theory. Feminists would argue that because women need to take care of their children they are often found in the secondary jobs sector. The secondary sector is where jobs have less security, lack of progression, low pay and part time hours. For many women this has to be a reality as they need to look after their children. Things are changing though, and many women do occupy jobs in the primary sector. For example there are more women in politics and senior positions like chief constables.

Another area of life in which women noticeably face patriarchy is the family. Women are given an expressive role in the family (Parsons), which means they are seen as the caregivers of the family. This is a role that has been ascribed to women for years and makes it difficult for women to break away from that role. Ann Oakley studied the amount of housework women do in her book, 'The sociology of housework', and she found that 80% of women have sole responsibility for childcare and housework compared to just 2% of men. Edgell also found that women do not get to make important decisions in the family and that men control women in this way. Pahl discovered that men also have more control over the finances in the family. This proves that the family is still an area that continues to oppress women. It is worth noting though that family life is changing and many men now take on an expressive role. Many women are the main breadwinner and the role of husbands and wives has changed to become more symmetrical. **[Mark: 10/10]**

This candidate expresses very good knowledge and understanding of the nature of patriarchy in society. There are two clear and distinct areas of social life, which are developed with sociological analysis, terminology, concepts and studies. This is why this candidate scores full marks.

Altruistic suicide	Émile Durkheim's term for suicide in societies where people see their own happiness as unimportant
Anomic suicide	Durkheim's term for suicide in societies where rapid change is occurring
Anomie	Term, first used by Durkheim, to describe a breakdown of social expectations and behaviour; later used differently by Merton to explain reactions to situations in which socially approved goals were impossible for the majority of the population to reach by legitimate means
Anthropocentric	The belief that humans have the right to exploit the environment for their own benefit
Anti-positivist	Rejecting the view that sociology can and should follow the methods and procedures of the natural sciences
Authenticity	The extent to which a historical document or other secondary source is real
Bedroom culture	Term used by Angela McRobbie and Jenny Garber to describe the way in which girls are more likely than boys to socialize with their friends in the home, rather than in streets or other public places
Bourgeoisie	Ruling class in capitalist society
Canteen culture	A term that refers to the occupational culture developed by the police
Capitalism	Term used to describe industrial society based on private ownership of property and businesses
Census	A questionnaire survey carried out by the government every 10th year on the whole population
Chivalry factor	Term used to suggest that the criminal justice system may treat women more leniently than men
Closed questions	Questions that require a specific reply, such as 'yes' or 'no'
Cluster sampling	The researcher selects a series of different places and then chooses a sample at random within the cluster of people within these areas
Collateral damage	Accidental and unintended damage
Comparative method	A method that involves comparing societies to find out key differences that might explain different social phenomena
Compensatory education	Diverting more educational funding to deprived areas
Complementarity	Type of **triangulation** in which different methods are combined to dovetail different aspects of an investigation (e.g. questionnaires are used to discover overall statistical patterns and participant observation is used to reveal the reasons for those patterns)
Consensus	General agreement
Conspicuous consumption	The idea that identity and status are dependent on material things such as designer labels and jewellery
Control group	In an experiment, the group not exposed to the **independent variable**
Corporate crime	Crimes committed by companies against employees or the public
Correlation	A statistical relationship between two or more social events
Covert participant observation	When the sociologist does not admit to being a researcher
Credibility	The degree to which a secondary source can be trusted
Crime Survey of England and Wales (CSEW)	An annual survey carried out by the Home Office
Criminogenic	Tending to produce crime or criminality

Cultural meanings	The ways in which things are interpreted differently in different societies
Cyber crime	Illegal acts using the internet
Dark figure	Amount of unknown crime that is never reported or recorded
Deforestation	The decline of forests caused by humans using the land and resources for other purposes
Demonization	Representing a particular group as deviant or evil
Dependent variable	A social phenomenon that changes in response to changes in another phenomenon
Desensitizing	Losing sensitivity to, for example, violence in the media
Deviancy amplification	When the action of the rule enforcers or media in response to deviance brings about an increase in the deviance
Deviant career	The various stages that a person passes through on their way to being seen as, and seeing themselves as, deviant
Difference feminism	Type of feminism that accepts that there are key differences in the experiences of different types of women, such as those from different classes, ethnicities and countries
Differential socialization	The theory that deviant behaviour is learned from, and justified by, family and friends
Domain assumptions	A world-view which is the result of socialization into a particular culture
Domestic labour	Housework
Dysfunctional	In functionalist theory, activities or institutions that do not appear to benefit society
Eco-centric view	The belief that damage to the environment ultimately damages the human race
Edgework	Originates from Stephen Lyng; refers to activities of young males which provide them with thrills derived from the real possibility of physical or emotional harm (e.g. stealing and then racing cars, and drug abuse)
Egoistic suicide	Durkheim's term for suicide in societies where people regard their individual happiness as very important
Empirical	Based on primary research
Entrepreneurial concern	Way of making money
Environmental crime prevention (ECP)	Right Realist idea that trivial anti-social acts should be clamped down on, otherwise whole areas will deteriorate as a sense of 'anything goes' develops (*see also* **zero tolerance**)
Ethnic cleansing	Forced and often violent removal of particular ethnic groups
Ethnographic research	Researching the natural everyday environment or context of whatever group is being studied
Experiment	A highly controlled situation in which researchers try to isolate the influence of each variable – rarely used in sociology
Experimental group	In an experiment, the group that is exposed to the **independent variable**
Facilitation	Type of **triangulation** in which one method is used to assist or develop the use of another method (e.g. when in-depth interviews are used to create questionnaire questions)
False class-consciousness	In Marxist analysis – the lack of awareness of being exploited
Feminization of the economy	Term used to describe the increase in service sector jobs that are often taken by women
Field experiment	An experiment undertaken in the community or in real life, rather than in a controlled environment
Focal concerns	Term used by Walter Miller to describe supposedly deviant values subscribed to by working-class youth

Folk devils	Individuals or groups of people associated with moral panics who are seen as troublemakers by the media
Functionalists	People who believe that the main cultural goal should be material success; functionalism is a doctrine that highlights purpose, practicality and utility and social order
Functions	Purposes
Genderquake	Term used by Helen Wilkinson to describe recent radical changes in gender roles
Gender-role socialization	Learning appropriate gender roles
Generalize	Being able to apply accurately the findings of research into one group to other groups
Genocide	Mass killing
Globalization	Process whereby national boundaries become less important
Going native	Researchers becoming too close to research participants and losing **objectivity**
Green crimes	Illegal acts that damage the environment
Hawthorne effect	Behaviour of research participants being affected as a result of the presence of researchers
Hegemonic	The dominant form of something
Hegemony	The ideas and values of the ruling class that dominate thinking in society
Homophobia	Hatred of gay people
Hyper-masculine	Extreme versions of typical male behaviour
Hypothesis	An initial plausible guess concerning the causal relationship between events
Hypothetico-deductive model	The research process associated with the physical sciences, used by **positivists** in sociology
Ideological function	Having the purpose of spreading ideas, values and beliefs
Ideological state apparatuses	A term used by the **neo-Marxist** writer Louis Althusser for those institutions that he claims exist to control the population through manipulating values (such as the media)
Ideology	Set of ideas and beliefs that justify actions
Illegitimate opportunity structures	Alternative, illegal ways of life, to which certain groups in society have access
Independent variable	In an experiment, the phenomenon that causes the **dependent variable** to change
Individualism	The pursuit of self-interest
Infrastructure	Term used by Marxists to describe the economic system or the way a society produces wealth
Institutional racism	Racism that is built into the normal practices of an organization
Interactionism	Shorthand term for **symbolic interactionism**
Interpretivist sociologists	Those whose approach to sociology and research emphasizes understanding society by exploring the way people see and interpret society, rather than by following traditional scientific analysis
Interview schedule	List of questions to be asked in an interview
Juvenile delinquency	Crimes committed by young people under 18
Labelling theory	A theory developed from **symbolic interactionism**, based on the view that deviance is merely a label applied to some people

Left Realism	A criminological theory which argues that crime is a real problem affecting working communities and is created principally by the inequalities in society, which capitalism causes. Left Realists argue that it is better to work within capitalism to improve people's lives than to attempt wholesale social change
Liberal feminists	Feminists who see society as **patriarchal** but suggest that women's opportunities are improving
Longitudinal research	Sociological research method involving studying a group over a long period of time
Macro theory	Way of looking at society which concentrates on how social structure determines individual behaviour
Manufactured risks	Threats to the ecosystem that are the result of the massive demand for consumer goods and the technology that underpins it
Marginalized	A sociological term referring to those who are pushed to the edge of society in cultural, status or economic terms
Marxist feminists/ feminism	Feminist theorists who base their theory on an adapted version of Marxism; a type of feminism that believes **patriarchy** is an ideological aspect of capitalism
Master status	When people are looked at by others solely on the basis of one type of act (good or bad) that they have committed, ignoring all other aspects of that person
Media literate	Able to look critically at the products of the media
Meritocratic	System of government or other administration in which people are appointed on merit
Metanarratives	A **postmodernist** term used to refer to the structural theories of Marxism and functionalism
Micro theories	Ways of explaining society that focus on how individuals interpret the social world
Moral codes	Sets of rules about what is right and wrong
Moral entrepreneur	Person who tries to create or enforce a rule
Moral panic	Outrage stirred up by the media about a particular group or issue
Moral regulation	The way societies control their members' values and beliefs
Neo-functionalist	Person who favours the updated version of the **functionalist** perspective
Neo-Marxism	Perspectives that update the ideas of Karl Marx
New Right	Perspective associated with the Conservative governments of Margaret Thatcher, favouring the free market and traditional ways of life
News values	Set of criteria used by the media to determine which events are newsworthy
Non-participant observation	Where the sociologist simply observes the group but does not seek to join in their activities
Non-random sampling	Methods of selecting a sample in which every member of the sample population does not have an equal chance of being in the sample
Non-response	Failure of respondents to return questionnaires or complete interviews
Objectification of women	Treating women as sexual objects
Objectivity	Being unbiased
Open sciences	Sciences concerned with the study of things we cannot see or sense directly
Operationalize	To define something in such a way that it can be measured
Over-deterministic	Idea that behaviour is completely controlled by one factor
Paradigm	A framework of thought which provides the way we approach and understand an issue
Participant observation	Research method in which the sociologist joins in with the group they are studying

Paternalistic	Patronizing approach that removes people's freedom to choose
Patriarchal	Benefiting men; male-dominated
Pilot survey	Small preliminary survey aiming to test the methodology before the full survey is undertaken
Polarization	Term used by Marx to describe how, in capitalist society, the rich get richer and the poor get poorer
Positivists	Those advocating an approach that supports the belief that the way to gain knowledge is by following the conventional scientific model
Postmodern	A different perspective on contemporary society, which rejects modernism and its attempts to explain the world through overarching theories. Instead, it suggests that there is no single, shared reality and focuses attention on the significance of the media in helping to construct numerous realities
Prescriptive	Proposing remedies and solutions
Primary deviance	The act of breaking a rule
Principle of falsification	The testing of an empirical model with the aim of showing it to be false
Proletariat	Exploited class in capitalist society, who sell their labour to the **bourgeoisie**
Purposive sampling	A sampling technique involving the researcher choosing individuals or cases that fit the nature of the research
Qualitative data	Data concerned with feelings, motives and experiences
Qualitative research	A general term for approaches to research that are less interested in collecting statistical data, and more interested in observing and interpreting the ways in which people behave
Quandary	Problem or source of confusion
Quota sampling	Where a representative sample of the population is chosen, using known characteristics of the population
Radical feminism	A type of feminism that believes that modern societies are **patriarchal** societies in which women are exploited and oppressed by men in all aspects of social life; radical feminists are feminist theorists (and usually political activists) who see men and male behaviour as the main cause of women's position in society
Random sampling	Where a **representative** sample of the population is chosen by entirely random methods
Rapport	Trusting relationship between researcher and respondent
Recidivism	Repeat offending
Relative deprivation	How deprived someone feels in relation to others, or compared with their own expectations
Reliable	Refers to the need for research to be strictly comparable (this is not a great problem with questionnaires and structured/**closed question** interviews, but can pose a real problem in observational research, because of the very specific nature of the groups under study)
Representative	A sample is representative if it is an accurate cross-section of the whole population being studied, which allows the researcher to **generalize** the results for the whole population
Research population	The whole group that the researcher is studying
Reserve army of labour	Term used by Marxists to describe certain groups who are moved in and out of work by the capitalist class as it suits them
Response rate	The proportion of the questionnaires that are returned (could also refer to the number of people who agree to be interviewed)
Right Realism	Perspective on crime that sees crime as an inevitable result of people's selfish, individualistic and greedy nature; associated with Wilson and the idea of **zero tolerance**
Role-playing	Term used by Erving Goffman to describe the way in which people are like actors, each playing a number of parts in social life

Sampling frame	A list used as the source for a **random sample**
Secondary data	Data already collected by someone else for their own purposes
Secondary deviance	The response to rule-breaking, which usually has greater social consequences than initial rule-breaking
Self	Sense of our own uniqueness and identity
Self-fulfilling prophecy	A prediction that makes itself become true
Self-report studies	Studies in which people are asked to write down the crimes they have committed over a particular period
Service sector	Jobs in retail, distribution and administration
Situational crime prevention (SCP)	An approach to crime that ignores the motivation for offending and instead concentrates on making it more difficult to commit crime
Snowball sampling	A sampling technique which involves finding and interviewing a person who fits the research needs and then asking them to suggest someone else who might be willing to be interviewed
Social action theory	Another name for **symbolic interactionism**; social action theories focus on how society is built up from people interacting with one another
Social construction	In this case, refers to the fact that statistics represent the activities of the people constructing the statistics rather than some objective reality
Social control	The ways in which a society directs the behaviour of its members
Social democratic perspective	View that favours investment in public services and a redistribution of wealth from the rich to the poor
Social desirability effect	Bias in research caused by respondents giving responses they think match the values of the researcher
Social fact	A term used by Durkheim to claim that certain objective 'facts' exist in society that are not influenced by individuals (e.g. the existence of marriage, divorce and work)
Social integration	The extent to which people feel they 'belong' to a society or social group
Social interaction	The act of coming together in social groups to socialise or to perform functions, for example, men and women interact to form families
Social policy	Has two meanings – can refer to government policy to solve social problems or the academic subject of studying social problems
Social problems	Social behaviours that are damaging to society
Social structure	The way a society is built up
Specialized division of labour	Division of work into a wide variety of tasks
Status frustration	According to Albert Cohen, this occurs when young men feel that they are unable to obtain status through conventional means such as school or employment. Cohen argues that it fuels delinquency
Stereotype	Commonly held, but exaggerated and often inaccurate, belief
Stigmatized	Labelled in a negative way
Stop and search	Police officers have powers to stop and search those they 'reasonably' think may be about to commit, or have committed, a crime; this power is used more against ethnic minority youth than white youth
Strain	Term used by Robert Merton and other **functionalists** to describe a lack of balance and adjustment in society
Stratified sampling	When the population under study is divided according to known criteria such as sex and age in order to make the sample more representative

Structuralist theory	Theory based on the idea that 'society' is a social fact or thing that exercises influence over the behaviour of individuals
Subcultures	Distinctive sets of values that provide an alternative to those of the mainstream culture
Subjective	Personal, based on individual values
Superstructure	Term used by Marxists to describe the parts of society that are responsible for socialization and the spreading of ideology
Surplus value	Marxist term used to describe the profits extracted by capitalists from the labour of the proletariat
Survey	A large-scale piece of quantitative research aiming to make general statements about a particular population
Symbolic interaction	The ways in which people act by interpreting things like other people's language and non-verbal communication
Symbolic interactionism	A theory derived from social psychology which argues that people exist in a social world based on symbols that people interpret and respond to – **labelling theorists** tend to substitute the term 'label' for 'symbol'
Symbolization	Associating the dress, hairstyles and music of a youth culture with trouble and violence
Systematic sampling	Where every nth name (for example, every 10th name) on a list is chosen
Techniques of neutralization	Justifications for our deviant actions
Transnational corporations	Businesses that operate globally – their brands and products are often consumed world-wide
Triangulation (multi-strategy research)	A term often used to describe the use of multiple methods (**qualitative** and quantitative) in research
Underclass	Term used by Charles Murray to describe a distinctive 'class' of people whose lifestyle involves seeking to take what they can from the state and living a life involving petty crime and sexual gratification
Urbanization	The process of moving to cities associated with industrialization
Validity	Refers to the problem of ensuring that the questions actually measure what the researcher intends them to measure
Value consensus	General agreement on core beliefs
Value free	Not letting personal views influence research
Value judgement	A biased judgement based on principles and beliefs
Value-laden	Inevitably based on personal values
Variable	A social phenomenon that changes in response to another phenomenon
Verstehen	Empathetic understanding – getting inside the head of research subjects and seeing and understanding the social world as they do
Victim (or victimization) survey	Surveys during which people are asked what crimes have happened to them over a particular period
Welfare dependency	Becoming reliant on state benefits
White-collar crime	Middle-class crimes committed by white-collar workers – bureaucrats, professionals, managers and so on
Zemiology	The study of harm
Zero tolerance	**Right Realist** approach to crime that argues that the police should aggressively tackle all types of crime and disorder rather than reacting only to serious crime

Index

Ackers, Ronald 19
Adler, Freda 27
African-Caribbean people, crime statistics of 30, 40
age fallacy 44
agents of social control 17
Althusser, Louis 67
'altruistic' suicide 75, 119
American Dream 6
'anomic' suicide 76, 119
anomie 4, 6, 44, 65, 75, 119
Anonymous 50
anthropocentric view of big business 52, 119
anti-positivist 70, 95, 119
anti-social subcultures 29
Atkinson, J. Maxwell 84
attachment 21
authenticity of the document 88, 119

Becker, Howard 16
bedroom culture 26, 119
belief 21
Bentham, Jeremy 56
Bigo and Guild 58
boundaries between legal and illegal behaviour
    changing values 5
    reaffirming the boundaries 4–5
    social cohesion 5
bourgeoisie 32, 119
Bowling, Ben 30–1, 42
Box, Stephen 51
Box, Steven 43
'broken windows', theory of 23

canteen culture 119
capitalism 7, 119
capitalist ruling class 32
capitalist societies, crime in 10–13
Carlen, Pat 27
Census 81, 119
Chambliss, William 10
Charlesworth, Simon 20
chivalry factor 26, 42, 119
class and crime, relationship between 34
    class background of offenders in the UK 34
class fallacy 44
class inequalities, crime and 10–11
'closed' questions 78, 119
Cloward, Richard 9
cluster sampling 83, 119
Cohen, Albert 8, 9, 35
Cohen, Stan 46, 55
collateral damage 55, 119
collective conscience 4
commitment 21
comparative method 75, 119
compensatory education 98, 119
complementarity 91, 119
conformity 6
consensus 4, 119

conspicuous consumption of goods 119
consumerism 10
control group 76, 119
control theories 21
coroners 84–5
corporate crime 7, 10–12, 34, 43, 119
correlations 74, 119
covert participant observation 17, 29, 91, 119
credibility of the document 88, 119
Crime Survey of England and Wales (CSEW) 36, 40–1, 62, 79, 119
Criminal Justice Acts 14
criminogenic values and practices 10, 12, 119
critical victimology 62–3
Croall, Hazel 11–12
Crown Prosecution Service 63
cultural meanings 85, 119
cultural transmission 120
cyber crimes 49–50, 120

dark figure 38, 54, 120
DDoS 50
deforestation 53, 120
delinquency 8–9
demonization 46, 120
dependent variable 76, 120
desensitizing children and teenagers 45, 120
deviancy amplification 18, 120
deviant career 18, 120
difference feminism 69, 120
differential controls 26–7
differential socialization 26, 120
disciplinary power 57
discrimination 17
Ditton, Jason 44
domain assumptions 97, 120
domestic labour 68–9, 120
dramatic fallacy 44
Duffy, James 44
Durkheim, Émile 4–5, 65
    boundaries between legal and illegal behaviour 4–5
    crime and deviance 4
    modern societies, crime rates of 4
    pre-industrial societies, crime rates of 4
    punishment 60
    suicide 74–6
dysfunctional 5, 120

eco-centric view of environmental harm 52, 120
economic reductionism 67
edgework 29, 120
'egoistic' suicide 75, 120
empirical 120
    data 12
    evidence 32
entrepreneurial concern 29, 120

environmental crime prevention (ECP) 23, 58, 120
ethnic cleansing 54, 120
ethnic differences in crime rates 30–4
    demographic explanations 30
    interpretivist critiques of the criminal justice system 30–1
    Marxist and neo-Marxist explanations 32–4
ethnographic research 20, 120
experiment 76–7, 85, 92, 120
experimental group 76, 120

facilitation 91, 120
false class-consciousness 66, 120
Felson, Richard 44
female offenders 26–7
feminism 26–7, 68–9, 72, 98–9
    difference 69
    evaluation 69
    liberal 68
    Marxist 68–9
    radical 69
feminization of poverty 27
feminization of the economy 68, 120
field experiments 85–6, 120
financial fraud 11
focal concerns 8, 120
folk devil 32, 46, 121
functionalism 4–7, 12, 60, 64, 72, 99
    evaluation 65
    social order 64, 75
functionalists 121
    explanations of crime and deviance 4–7, 35
    sociological perspectives 100
functions 121

Garber, Jenny 26
gender differences in crime rates
    explanations for lower female crime rate 26–7
    masculinity and 28–9
genderquake 68, 121
gender-role socialization 28, 121
generalize 82, 121
genocide 54, 121
global crime 48–51
globalization 67, 73, 100, 121
    crime and 48–51, 55
'glocal' trade 49
going native 97, 121
Gordon, David 10, 32, 35
Gouldner, Alvin 96–7
green crime 52–3, 121
    policing 53

hacktivism 50
Hall, Stuart 14
Hamilton, V. Lee 55
Hammersley, Martyn 91
Harvey, David 67
Hawthorne effect 77, 121

hegemonic masculine value system 28, 121
hegemony 32, 121
Heidensohn, Frances 26–7
Hirschi, Travis 21, 35
Hitchens, Chris 54
Holdaway, Simon 30
homophobia 54, 121
Houchin, Roger 34
human rights, crime against 54–5
hyper-masculine 33, 121
hypothesis 75, 121
hypothetico-deductive model 92, 121

identity theft 49
ideological function 14, 32, 42, 121
ideological state apparatus 10, 121
ideology 10, 44, 52, 66, 68–9, 100, 121
illegal drugs trade 49
illegitimate opportunity structure 9, 121
illegitimate or criminal global economy 48
independent variable 76, 121
individualism 4, 10, 24, 121
industrialization 72
infrastructure 10, 66–7, 121
ingenuity fallacy 44
innovation 6
institutional racism 30, 42, 54, 121
interactionism 41, 121
interactionist explanations of crime and deviance 16–19
    agents of social control 17
    definitions of deviance 16
    deviancy amplification 18
    interpretation of deviance 16
    negotiation of justice 17
    primary deviance and secondary deviance 17–18
    social construction of deviance 16
interpretivists 30, 41, 70, 76
    preference for qualitative methods 97
    research methods 84–91
interpretivist sociology 95, 121
interview schedule 77, 79, 86, 121
involvement 21
IP theft 50

juvenile delinquency 8, 121

Katz, Jackson 29
Kelman, Herbert 55
King, Martin Luther 5
Kuhn, Thomas 94

labelling theory 9, 13–14, 35, 41, 71, 121
    evaluation of 18–19
laboratory experiments 76–7
Lawrence, Stephen 30
Lea, John 24, 41, 43, 47
Lees, Sue 63

Left Realism 35, 56, 122
Left Realists 13, 47, 101
    explanations of crime and deviance 24–5, 32, 35
    social and community crime prevention 58–9
    solutions to crime 25
Lemert, Edwin 17
liberal feminism 68, 101, 122
liberation theory 27
Lizard Squad 50
longitudinal character of observation studies 91
longitudinal research 77, 122
Lyng, Stephen 29

MacPherson Report 30, 42
macro theory 64, 66, 122
Mandela, Nelson 5
manufactured risks 52, 73, 122
marginalization 24
marginalized 24, 122
Marsland, David 20
Marxism 60–1, 66–7, 72, 92, 99
    evaluation 66–7
Marxist explanations of crime and deviance 10–13, 35
    class inequalities, effect of 10–11
    ideological state apparatus 10
Marxist feminism 68–9, 122
masculinity
    changing nature in Sunderland 29
masculinity and crime 29–30
masculinized-driven violence 9
master status 17, 122
materialism 10
Matza, David 9
McLaughlin, Eugene 54
McRobbie, Angela 26, 47
meaning 8, 45, 49–51, 65, 70–1, 84–7, 89, 95
mechanical solidarity 4
media as a possible cause of crime 44–5
media literate 45, 122
Menezes, Jean Charles de 63
meritocracy 122
Merton, Robert 6–7, 13, 35
    different forms of behaviour or adaptations 6
Messerschmidt, James 28
metanarratives 72, 122
micro theories 70–1, 122
Miller, Walter 8–9
modernism 72–3
money laundering 50
moral codes 64, 122
moral entrepreneurs 46, 122
moral panic 46–7, 122
moral regulation 75, 122
Morrison, David 45
mugging 14
Muncie, John 47
Murray, Charles 20, 35

neo-functionalist 45, 122
neo-Marxism 14, 67, 122
neo-Marxist explanations of crime and deviance 14–15, 35
    vs traditional Marxists 14
New Criminology 14–15, 35
New Right sociology 100, 122
news values 44, 122
non-participant or direct observation 89, 122
non-random sampling methods 83, 122
non-response 78, 122

objectification of women 28, 122
objectivity 74, 122
Office for National Statistics (ONS) 62
official crime statistics (OCS) 30, 36–7
    Crime Survey of England and Wales (CSEW) 40–1
    effect of victim reporting 39
    Marxist critique of 42–3
    media as a possible cause of crime 44–5
    problems associated with crime statistics 37
    reliability and validity of crime statistics 37–8
    theoretical problems 41–3
    trends and patterns in criminal activity 36
official statistics 81
Ohlin, Lloyd 9
online scams 49
open sciences 94, 122
operationalizing 53, 122
organic solidarity 4
over-deterministic 65, 69, 122

panopticon 56–8
paradigms 94, 122
Parks, Rosa 5
participant observation 89–91, 122
paternalistic 26, 123
patriarchal society 26, 123
personal documents 88
Phillips, Coretta 30–1, 42
pilot survey 78, 123
polarization of people 67, 123
police fallacy 44
policing 41
Popper, Karl 92–3
positivists 37, 74, 123
    research methods 74–81
postmodernism 72–3
postmodern 52
    societies 73
poverty, feminization of 27
prejudice 17
prescriptive science of society 96, 123
prevention and control of crime 56–61
primary deviance 17, 123
principle of falsification 93, 123
prison, pros and cons of 59–60

proletariat 66, 123
punishment 59–60
   pros and cons of prison 59–60
   sociological perspectives on 60–1
purposive sampling 83, 123

qualitative data 84–8, 90–1, 123
qualitative research 83, 123
quandary 33, 123
questionnaires 77–8
quota sampling 83, 123

racial crime 14
radical feminism 69, 101, 123
random sampling 82–3, 123
rapport 87, 123
rational choices 27
rational choice theory 21
rebellion 6
recidivism 60, 123
Reiman, Jeffrey 11
Reiner 35, 45
relative deprivation 24, 123
reliability 74, 123
representative 36, 40, 81–3, 88, 123
research population 82, 123
reserve army of labour 68, 123
response rate 79, 123
restitutive justice 60
retreatism 6
retribution 23, 60
Rex, John 21
Right Realism 35, 56, 123
Right Realists explanations of crime
   and deviance 20–1, 35
   main aspects 20–1
   perspectives on social policy and
     sociology 100–1
   right realist schemes to prevent and
     control crime 22–3
ritualism 6
role-playing 71, 123

sampling 82–3
sampling frame 82, 124
Schwendinger, Herman 54
science
   interpretivist sociology and 95
   paradigms and 94
   postmodernists and 95
scientific realism 94
secondary data 40, 77, 81, 88, 91, 124
secondary deviance 17, 124
self 70, 124
self-fulfilling prophecies 17, 46, 71, 124

self-report questionnaires 79
self-report studies 42, 124
service sector 68, 124
Sewell, Tony 33
sexist 26
sex trafficking 49
situational crime prevention (SCP) 22,
   56, 124
smuggling 49
snowball sampling 83, 124
social action theory 14, 70–1, 124
   socialization and identity 70–1
social and community crime
   prevention 58–9
social construction 41, 124
social control 4, 65, 124
social democratic perspective 101, 124
social desirability effect 97, 124
social experiments 85–6
social facts 75, 124
social integration 65, 75, 124
social interaction 70, 124
socialization 64
social media and surveillance 57
social policy 22, 25, 100–1, 124
social problems 124
social structures 4, 124
social surveys 77
sociology on policy 100–1
Soothill, Keith 44
specialized division of labour 65, 124
state crime 34, 54–5
status frustration 8, 124
stereotype 42, 124
stigmatized 17, 124
stop and search 18, 124
strain 6, 8–9, 124
stratified sampling 83, 124
structuralist theory of crime 4, 125
structured interviews 79–80
subcultural delinquent behaviour,
   types of 9, 33, 35
subcultural explanations of crime and
   deviance 8–9
   Cloward, Richard 9
   Cohen, Albert 8
   criticisms of 9
   Miller, Walter 8–9
   Ohlin, Lloyd 9
subcultures 24, 125
subjective 53, 70, 73, 88, 95, 125
superstructure 10, 66, 125
surplus value 66, 125
surveillance 56–8
survey of crime victimization 36, 125

symbolic interaction 70, 125
symbolization 46, 125
systematic sampling 82, 125

Tatchell, Peter 5
Taylor, Steve 88
techniques of neutralization 55, 125
terrorist attacks 5
Thornton, Sarah 47
'three strikes and you are out'
   policy 23
Tomlinson, Sally 21
transnational corporations 48, 125
triangulation 91, 125
triple quandary theory 33

underclass 20, 125
underclass theory 20
unstructured interviews 86–7
urbanization 72, 125

validity of OCS 37, 125
value consensus 4, 125
value-free sociology 96, 125
   critique of 96–9
value judgements 46, 91, 125
value-laden 125
vandalism 14, 23, 40
variable 76, 86, 94, 125
Venkatesh, Sudhir 9, 89–90
verstehen 95, 125
victimization 24
victim (or victimization) survey of
   inner-city London 24, 125
victims of crime 62–3

Walby, Sylvia 44
Walklate, Sandra 27, 63
Weber, Max 96
welfare dependency 20, 125
White, Rob 52
white-collar crime 7, 10–12, 34,
   43, 125
Wilkins, Les 18
Wilkinson, Helen 68
Wilkinson, Richard 12
Wilson, James 23, 58
Winlow, Simon 29
working-class crime 14, 35

Young, Jock 24, 41, 43, 46, 62

zemiology 51, 125
zero tolerance policing strategy 23, 125